Praise for *American Manifesto*

"Short, specific, and droll. It is very much worth reading, for ideas about the next stage in the world's recovery from failed, weak, and in other ways troubled media systems." —JAMES FALLOWS, *The Atlantic*

"Bob Garfield speaks truth not just to power, but to the dangerously disempowered. Unflinchingly direct yet courageously sympathetic." —DOUGLAS RUSHKOFF, author of *Present Shock* and *Team Human*

"In *American Manifesto*, Bob Garfield bares our national soul, and it's hellishly dark. We've divided ourselves by everything under the sun, eroding the idea of America as the common home of the many. With wit, passion, and insight, Garfield dissects the problem and issues a call to action. He will convince you that it's time to get out the door." —THOMAS E. PATTERSON, Bradlee Professor of Government and the Press at Harvard University and author of *How America Lost Its Mind*

"In the vast, bland American wasteland of homogenized, regurgitated media, there is a lone, heroic taco truck. Bob Garfield is that taco truck. Nourishing. Defiant. Also very smart and very brave. *American Manifesto* is his spicy masterpiece." —ALEC BALDWIN

"Garfield's (*Bedfellows*, 2012, etc.) manifesto stands out from those already published . . . An interesting manifesto that will incite debate." —*Kirkus Reviews*

"Garfield offers practical advice on how to transform outrage into positive action. Fans of his Peabody Award–winning public radio program, *On the Media*, will recognize Garfield's bold yet grounded humor, while his trenchant analysis and surprisingly hopeful vision will motivate readers to pay attention and get involved." —*Booklist*

ALSO BY BOB GARFIELD

Waking Up Screaming from the American Dream
And Now a Few Words from Me
The Chaos Scenario
Bedfellows
Can't Buy Me Like

American Manifesto

SAVING DEMOCRACY FROM
VILLAINS, VANDALS,
AND OURSELVES

BOB GARFIELD

COUNTERPOINT
Berkeley, California

The Library of Congress has cataloged the hardcover as follows:
Names: Garfield, Bob, author.
Title: American manifesto : saving democracy from villains, vandals, and
   ourselves / Bob Garfield.
Description: First hardcover edition. | Berkeley, California : Counterpoint, 2020.
Identifiers: LCCN 2019017896 | ISBN 9781640092808
Subjects: LCSH: Identity politics—United States. | Polarization (Social
   sciences)—Political aspects—United States. | Political culture—United States.
Classification: LCC JK1764 .G369 2020 | DDC 306.20973—dc23
LC record available at https://lccn.loc.gov/2019017896

Paperback ISBN: 978-1-64009-461-1

Cover design by Richard Ljoenes
Book design by Jordan Koluch

COUNTERPOINT
2560 Ninth Street, Suite 318
Berkeley, CA 94710
www.counterpointpress.com

Printed in the United States of America

For my children, and my children's children

This quiet sail is as a noiseless wing
To waft me from distraction.

—LORD BYRON

CONTENTS

INTRODUCTION

R ead this book. Commit it to memory. Tear out the pages and swallow them. Chew carefully, but hurry. Not to say necessarily that the political situation in this country will so deteriorate that ICE expands its roundups to political dissidents or the dangerously informed, but never say "never." There are scoundrels loose in Washington, D.C.—and Madison, Wisconsin, and Atlanta, Georgia, and wherever dark money lurks—systematically undermining the institutions of justice and civil freedoms. It may be deemed an extreme view that tyranny is upon us, but also let us not be lulled into complacency. Back in the early '60s, when Barry Goldwater was considered insanely far right, the Arizona senator declared, "Extremism in the defense of liberty is no vice." He was worried about the Russkies.

Yeah. Me, too. But not in a commie way. More of in a fascist way, with domestic stooges doing the dirty work.

This book is a cry for help in three parts. The dry way of describing it: "An examination of the tragic confluence of the American preoccupation with identity and the catastrophic disintegration of mass media, yielding a society that may be irretrievably fractured unless we act now." A less dry way of putting it: "Run for your life. We're being Dumptied." As in Humpty, the self-satisfied jumbo egg that once sat atop a big, beautiful wall and wound up in countless irreparable pieces.

Take note: I am not speaking of Trumpty Dumpty. The greatest threat we face is not from a rogue president, but from ourselves.

The frightening evidence is all around us, but maybe none more troubling than the survey results that show millennials shopping for other forms of government. The 2018 Democracy Project, undertaken jointly by the Freedom House, the George W. Bush Institute, and the Penn Biden Center for Diplomacy and Global Engagement at the University of Pennsylvania, asked fourteen hundred adults about the importance of democracy as our form of government. Among respondents aged twenty-nine or younger, only 39 percent said "absolutely important." Overall, only 60 percent of those polled expressed absolute adamancy. When asked if America is in "real danger of becoming a nondemocratic, authoritarian country," overall, 50 percent said yes.

Half of us are in fear of democracy's collapse? How in the world did we get *there*?

Well, I have a detailed answer to that question, and then I further presume to prescribe a solution—a solution that has little to do with the actions of government, quite a bit to do with the imperatives of the marketplace, and most of all to do with you, the citizen. So, yes, *American Manifesto* is a call to action, but it requires maybe a more challenging commitment: to be prepared to discard, or at least reconsider, aspects of your own personal orthodoxy, your assumptions, your affinities, and maybe even one or two articles of faith. Because the time for narrow interests, and the time for delicacy, has passed. This is an emergency. It's time for all the king's horses and all the king's men to get fucking busy. Please note also: I am *not* inciting a revolution. I am outlining a de-devolution.

Now, you might rightly wonder who the hell I am to prescribe anything. I am not a political scientist. I am not a sociologist. Or a psychologist, neuroscientist, or philosopher. I do have one PhD (honorary) in exchange for dispensing twenty minutes of advice to a stadium full of college graduates who just wanted to get out of the sun and commence moving back in with their folks. But an honorary degree is like an auxiliary police badge; you don't have to go to the academy to earn it. Until very recently, I wasn't even much acquainted with the scholarly literature on the subject I presume herewith to address.

What I am is a serial eyewitness to and chronicler of developments in society, technology, politics, and media. In other words: a journalist, drawing my livelihood for decades from reporting, contextualizing, connecting dots, and a fair amount of just plain gawking. And it so happens that a pretty significant part of my beat, in almost every permutation of my diverse journalistic career, has been the search for identity—whether in the coverage of identity politics, nationalism, social media, advertising, pop culture, or (for many years on the radio and in print) the quixotic tilts of ordinary Americans trying to achieve the pinnacle of Maslow's (and Horatio Alger's and Thomas Jefferson's) pyramid to "make something of themselves." It's an eclectic resume, burnished by the mere fact of having walked the planet since 1955 and observing my ass off along the way. I may not have tenure at a prestigious private university, but I can observe like nobody's business. And that is precisely what I propose to do here.

The story starts with a little bit of political anthropology, how the relentless American quest for identity has atomized the nation of *e pluribus unum*, at grave risk to its core values, social order, and democracy itself. Much of this is the consequence of well-intentioned multiculturalism, but fission in the nucleus of society triggered a dangerous chain reaction and—physics being what it is—an equal and opposite reaction. Also known as backlash. That is to say that the politics of identity antagonized the right until finally being seized upon by the right. They have expropriated the raw power of victimhood, which has yielded creeping authoritarianism, nationalism, xenophobia, bizarre conspiracy theories, and incendiary presidential Big Lies. So, while the sulfur of fascism fouls the air, across the ideological spectrum our politics have devolved into blind rage. Not to put too fine a point on it, American society as a functioning democracy could be doomed.

Which may even be an understatement because, in part II, we'll contemplate a parallel phenomenon that exponentially exacerbates the crisis, rendering us very likely super-double-doomed. Namely, the effect of the digital revolution on the mass media and all that flows from not having a functioning Fourth Estate.

Digital technology has given us smart fridges, Airbnb, artificial intelligence, *Fortnite*, and E-ZPass, which is swell. These are the bounty of technological innovation, and who's to complain—unless you're a tollbooth operator who's been E-Z laid off. Digital revolution, like any other, has in some quarters left blood running in the gutters—most especially in the media sector. It's not just that a few arrogant and hidebound publishing and broadcasting incumbents have been pushed aside by savvy innovators steeped in the culture of code, foosball, and Series B funding rounds. Media have been "disrupted" like the *Hindenburg* was "disrupted." A three-century-old mass-media model has been blown to smithereens, and the surviving journalistic fragments are not only too poor to adequately watchdog the government, but also algorithmically segregated from huge swaths of the electorate. O, the humanity.

Finally, in part III, the manifesto itself.

Nanopolitics and nanomedia are each individually ruinous. The explosive combination has concussed American democracy to the brink. We have had a great fall, and all the king's horses and all the king's men—like the Charlottesville police—are just staring blankly at the chaos. If the democracy were functioning properly, if the levers of government were not controlled by a few hundred or so white men—bought and paid for by political interests—who have long since abandoned the supposed core values of their party in exchange for money and power, this section would be about policy and governance. It would be about campaign-finance law, Senate rules, gerrymandering, voter suppression, and civil rights. But the few in power have systematically exploited the tools of democracy to subvert democracy. They have hijacked their party and the government itself, and even if they are voted out of office, the damage to due process, honesty, equity, constitutional verity, and planetary survival will require a generation, or more, to repair. And so it falls to outside forces to restore principle and equilibrium to the society. Not foreign forces, not One World Government or Justin Trudeau or Bono. No, the outside force on which we depend is us. The government is supposed to be the people's fortress, but we find ourselves walled off, on the wrong side of the moat. Which is not a bad metaphor, but permit me to return to my central one. The manifesto outlines the remedy, perhaps the last remaining remedy, for hyperfragmentation. It enumerates six planks, six varied spheres of activity—one economic, one regulatory, one militant, one educational, one inspirational, one sweet Kumbaya—for putting our fractured Humpty Dumpty of a society back together again.

And so we must. And so we shall.

PART I

THE BIG WHO

1

Pokémon Go: Inner-Self Edition

In the summer of 2016, through the miraculous convergence of smartphones, geo-mapping, and augmented reality, millions and millions of Americans wandered around city and countryside, hill and dale, in search of Pikachu, Eevee, Ditto, and 150 other Pokémon avatars. It was actually a global phenomenon, a massive multiplayer scavenger hunt in which players obsessively sought colorful new characters to achieve success.

The American hunters, however, had a huge advantage. Because character search is what we do, and always have.

The search for identity is a general earthly impulse, but here in the USA, it is something like a national sport—from the goth table in the high school cafeteria to the cult of Apple to khakied Charlottesville brandishers of tiki torches. Distinct identity is how we define our leaders (Abraham Lincoln splitting logs, Teddy Roosevelt charging up San Juan Hill, JFK's youthful vigor, Connecticut-born

George W. Bush "clearing brush"); our icons (Bogey, Charlie Chaplin, Muhammad Ali); our brands (Marlboro, Levi's, Subaru); our music (country, hip-hop, Christian, metal). And, OMG, sports. It's not just that we affiliate ourselves, sometimes deeply and for life, with collegiate or professional teams. Millions of us feel the need to announce those affiliations on our clothing and car bumpers. Whether we are discussing Cubs vs. Sox, sneakers, religion, the Missouri Compromise, or the relative merits of Ginger and Mary Ann, no sphere of American endeavor can be viewed separately from the expressions of identity that are both its components and its product. Are there vanity plates in, say, Belgium? Is there anywhere but the USA where the driver behind you is informed ILVTOFU?

Not just pointing fingers here. I, myself, have over the decades devoted an enormous amount of thought and energy to divining my true essence and projecting an accurate, attractive image of myself in matters of style, political leanings, and general deportment. This from a very early stage. At the age of five, there was a soft woolen shirt with an unsightly striped collar that I nonetheless wanted to wear every day, because to me it just screamed "ME." In sixth grade, it embarrasses me to reveal, I did my best to alter my gait to affect a certain insouciance, even though I was easily the most souciant twelve-year-old in the Cynwyd School. (If I recall correctly, the stride was vaguely hip-swinging and heel-intensive.) It did not work, and it did not last. A Nehru jacket followed. Then hippieish long hair, wire-rimmed glasses, and a raffish vest (harvested, oy vey, from my bar mitzvah suit). Then the bohemian high school years—all baggy, thrift-store woolens, setting me very much apart in the cafeteria from the greasers, the jocks, the potters in leotards, and the theater dorks with their top hats and unicycles. Then, in college, the studied carelessness of any sensitive Ivy League intellectual— except I went to Penn State, and the pipe I affected made me no more well read. Then, as a young adult, a turn prep-ward. And now, finally, equal parts dad jeans and Eurotrash. My musical, literary, cinematic, and political tastes have been significantly less volatile but also not set in stone. Under the influence of certain offspring, there is suddenly more hip-hop than rock in my ear.

This stuff doesn't just happen; it's a series of choices emerging from a little bit of exploration, a little bit of observation, a little bit of reflection, a little bit of reinvention, a little bit of self-actualization, and along the way a whole shit-ton of hand-wringing. Because, after all, I'm the only me I have, and this sort of core understanding and persona renovation do not come easily. Polonius sagely counseled Laertes, "To thine own self be true." For whatever reason, Laertes did not reply, "Thanks, Pop. I'm headed to England. Maybe I'll locate him there."

Because that self can be elusive—although Laertes could have just checked out his own Facebook page.

Consider this: According to a 2016 poll by the political advocacy group Rad Campaign, 96 percent of Americans don't trust social media sites with their private information. A Pew Research Center poll from the same year found that 86 percent of Americans had taken steps to remove or mask their digital footprints. Yet 79 percent of American adults reported using Facebook, up from 72 percent only one year earlier. There, in mind-boggling numbers—no matter which prying governments, marketers, potential employers, or criminals might be watching—we share the latest on our families, our activities, our locations, ours plans, our kids, our likes and dislikes, our politics, our random thoughts, and photos of our freaking meals. Why? Because the accumulation of these personal features is an expression of self. As

Mark Zuckerberg candidly (for once) observed, "they're keeping up with their friends and family, but they're also building an image and identity for themselves, which in a sense is their brand."

Around the year A.D. 100, the Greek stoic philosopher Epictetus counseled, "Learn first who you are, and then adorn yourself accordingly." Maybe, or maybe as George Bernard Shaw would have it, vice versa: "Life isn't about finding yourself. Life is about creating yourself." Rocking a Nehru jacket has nothing to do with Nehru; it's all about projection. The evidence for this can be found in any Catholic girls' school, where the enforced conformity of the school uniform is often subverted by distinctive bracelets, barrettes, hair bands, and shoelaces. Or, as we are reminded by scholars Susan O. Michelman and Joanne B. Eicher, women in Nigerian Kalabari societies have embraced fashion explicitly to communicate advances in their social and political clout, a textile taxonomy of status approximately like the insignias on military uniforms.

Personal brand building is not a new development. Fashion and decor are and have for all of modernity been signals as to the nature of the inhabitant. In the industrial age, this has gradually and often absurdly extended to almost every category of consumer product, as marketers of cars, beer, cigarettes, and other goods realized that their products were doing double duty as badges of the consumer's particular tastes and values—whereupon the brands themselves began advertising not about the intrinsic properties of the goods but of the statement they made to the outside world. Marlboros were evidence of rugged individualism, Budweiser was for patriots, Camel Filters and Stroh's beer and Dr Pepper purchases meant flipping the bird at The Man, a Mercedes was proof of success and a VW was proof of levelheadedness, a badge of conspicuously inconspicuous consumption.

Yes, that is a paradox heaped upon a paradox: the expression of your unique persona through the display of mass-marketed goods—most emphatically demonstrated by the faddish popularity in the 1980s of Members Only racer jackets. They were a ubiquitous badge of (supposed) exclusivity, available only to the rarefied few tens of millions who could spare the $11 to purchase one damn near anywhere. Even the most lauded TV commercial in history— Ridley Scott's iconic Super Bowl ad "1984"—depicted an athletic young woman representing Apple as she liberated an audience of slack-mouthed zombies from the spell of a bellicose info-tyrant Big Brother. At the time, he was meant to symbolize IBM. Apple subsequently moved on to demonize Microsoft, and now Google, as the entity for customers to define themselves in heroic opposition to.

The dark art of brand imaging evolved into a science called demographics, wherein marketers cross-referenced consumer-goods preferences with media choices and neighborhoods to divine the likeliest targets and conduits for their advertising messages. A cellophane-wrapped beef-stick person was very likely also to be a budget-beer person and highly unlikely to be a *Town & Country* subscriber. First zip codes, then zip+4, became proxies for the values and lifestyles of the addressee and, of course, ultimately for the persona of the person dwelling therein. Billions of marketing dollars were divvied up among such market segments as "Blue Blood Estates," "Shotguns & Pickups," and "White Picket Fences." In the consumer society, it was the perfect symbiosis: marketers playing to the self-images of their prospects, and consumers all too eager to purchase exactly the right good to express their true natures . . . or to reengineer them. On the latter possibility, think Olivia Newton John in *Grease* or Melanie Griffith in *Working Girl*. Or Truman Capote's indelible Holly Golightly in *Breakfast at Tiffany's*.

So much of this data is simply shorthand. In the hoary days of olde—say, 1996—houseguests or dates might get a fix on the hosts by performing a quick scan of the bookshelves, record collection, decor, and, yes, whatever was in the fridge and the driveway. This was the proto-Facebook—primitive, but not unrevealing. (Barry Manilow and Dr. Wayne Dyer? Really? *Miracle Whip?!*) But of course, in today's Big Data world, the quick domicile once-over and even the behavioral approximations from the likes of Simmons Market Research Bureau, Claritas, and Stanford Research are downright quaint. Nowadays actual data gleaned from individuals' online behavior offers granular detail about the personal life, specific interests, and actual behaviors of the IP address holder. When databases are overlaid, the algorithms and their human proprietors know more about you than your mother, your spouse, and perhaps even your own careless self. In 2018, such data brokers as Oracle, Acxiom, and Experian—sometimes called "privacy death stars"—sold advertisers about $4 billion worth of, ahem, consumer insights. The *Financial Times* recently documented the case of a Belgian fellow named Paul-Olivier Dehaye, who was the subject of an alert to advertisers on a hot June day because—according to the data tea leaves—Dehaye has an overactive bladder.

That is how Cambridge Analytica used fifty million Facebook profiles to play havoc with the 2016 presidential election and precisely why people express fear about social media platforms; we are vulnerable to privacy invasion on an Orwellian scale, and yet we persist in divulging our most intimate details. In *Rhetoric*, Aristotle called this "compulsion," one of his seven causes of human action. However, it is not merely human instinct—embedded in the very biochemistry of our cellular activity—but animal instinct; Charles Darwin wrote about it in 1874. Nowadays, in both contexts, fundamental self-expression is labeled *signaling*, which according to the editors of *Animal Signals*, a hefty tome about signaling and signal design in animal communication

> is about blackbirds defending their territories, peacocks inform- ing peahens of their qualities, and about wild dogs telling about their aggressive intentions. It is about salmon and blueberry ad- vertising their ripeness, as partners or prey. And it is about hu- man language, and information traveling across cell walls within a body. In sum, signals may communicate qualities, status, and intentions of entities at various levels.... Animal communication has also important interfaces with numerous other disciplines, such as evolutionary biology, molecular biology, neuroscience, medicine, linguistics, cognitive science, chemistry and physics.

You aren't mistaken. In the introduction to their anthology, the zoologists Yngve Espmark, Trond Amundsen, and Gunilla Rosenqvist did indeed mention "blueberry." If you were a bit despondent that your preoccupation with projecting an identity is little more than a bestial instinct, yes, it gets worse. Because plants do it, too. In their 2010 paper "Identity Recognition and Plant Behavior," scientists Richard Karban and Kaori Shiojiri describe "different behaviors based on identity.... Plants may differentiate self from non-self and alter their morphologies in response to cues from these two types of sources. Plants appeared to recognize their own roots and to grow fewer and shorter roots when they contacted self roots compared to non-self roots."

It's a nature thing.

No wonder then that the impulse to project an image to the out- side world via digital platforms is, for most of us, simply irresistible, trumping serious misgivings about privacy risk and even personal security. This is why some peacocks get mates and some get eaten by feral dogs. In more ways than one, and with a nod to media scholar Neil Postman, we are selfing ourselves to death. As a society, and increasingly as a species, we are playing a continuous game of *Pokémon Go*—the twist being that we are not merely *following* the clues in search of our elusive selves; we are leaving them, too.

The perils of identity obsession do not end with the incautious display of plumage. All this inward looking and outward projecting has implications for the body politic. More on this subject to follow, but let us momentarily consider multiculturalism. On the face of it, the multiculti world is the apotheosis of liberal democracy, the recognition and celebration of the diverse ethnic, religious, racial, and national constituents of a just, mindful society whose whole exceeds the sum of its parts. It is a vision of vanishing hatreds, joyous comingling, social justice, and the rich infusion of cultural treasures. Kumbaya! Who needs a melting pot when we can have paella?

Sure enough, in the thirty years since multiculturalism began gaining traction, the benefits have been piling up: ethnic pride, less bland and homogenous pop culture, greater exposure to and therefore less fear of exotic "others"—a phenomenon also known as "tolerance," which has to be the lowest bar for social contentment ever conceived. But also piling up, as predicted by Arthur Schlesinger's cautionary 1991 polemic *The Disuniting of America*, are two troubling unintended consequences:

- The fragmentation and refragmentation of the populace into ever smaller interest groups, each with its own discrete desires . . . and grievances.
- The dilution of our pluralistic founding national identity *e pluribus unum*—from many, one—the great American

alloy poured from the melting pot. Not just peeved sub-group backlash, but broad nativist backlash, with ugly fascist currents, to the multiculturation of the country they claim no longer to recognize. Which has given us Trump. Which is, as the philosophers said, a fucking nightmare.

In America, right now, sure enough, identity perilously rears its head. As we shall see forthwith, the politics and societal shifts of the past sixty years—including the triumphs of the oppressed and the long-overdue beneficiaries of constitutional equity—have delivered a bounty, and also an inevitable backlash: a put-upon, dwindling majority of white Americans who lament the gradual erosion of their values, their way of life, and their primacy in American society. Their grievances have been smoldering for decades, but as the modern values of liberal democracy have increasingly become institutionalized in the halls of government, on campuses, in media, in places of worship, and even at work, they've felt decreasingly safe even voicing their frustration aloud. Meantime, the elements of reaction, once the province of an isolated fringe, have edged more and more mainstream. What used to be confined to the wingnuts of the John Birch Society has become prime-time programming on Fox News, not to mention the rest of the exploding right-wing media sector. The line between conservatism and corrosive ethno-nationalism has become ever fuzzier, and in this environment—incited by the lies and hateful dog whistles of a gilded golf-resort demagogue—they have found themselves and elements of the so-called alt-right, the (literally) rebranded white-identity movement, a legion of misogynist Gamergate bros, racists, militant Christians, and the fearful victims of globalism in rural and postindustrial America coalesced as a formidable coalition. And why?

Well, because they were endowed by their creator with certain inalienable rights, including the pursuit of happiness, which they understand doesn't necessarily guarantee riches, but definitely doesn't sound like being a Walmart greeter. You heard all the pundits on election night 2016. Trump voters chafed at having their destiny snatched from them. I'd say what was taken from them was taken by technology, climate change, and global redistribution of manufacturing—not some sinister Mexican or Muslim or international Jew. But they don't see it that way. They think—and not entirely without justification—that they're victims of the world's biggest bait and switch, robbing them of not only their chance to pursue happiness, but also their very identity. Because when you used to make $45 an hour down at the auto-parts plant and now you're driving an airport shuttle for $12, what does that make you? When your whiteness and your Christianity have gotten you maxed out on three credit cards and a mosque is going up down by the middle school, whose fault is that? When there's someone named Courtni at the next urinal, who are you? For decades they've been facing that conundrum, seething, resenting, blaming, fantasizing about a return to an America that reflected their values and resembled their group photos. And now their greatest fantasy has come to pass. Trump and his cabal are in power. What they call "political correctness"—and what I call the Bill of Rights—is under siege. They hear about "white privilege" and they're like, "Yeah. I'll have more of that." They have resurrected their identity through their very rage. And this is their moment. And they will have their revenge.

The day after Donald Trump was elected, the headline on the website of the libertarian publication *Reason* summarized the trenchant, if self-satisfied, analysis of a young writer named Robby Soave: "Trump Won Because Leftist Political Correctness Inspired a Terrifying Backlash," which the site suggested would explain "what every liberal who didn't see this coming needs to understand." Arrogant.

Reductive. And more obviously true with every passing day. With every executive order dismantling regulations and civil liberties, with every attack on minorities and every *Heil* Trump.

All wrapped, of course, in declarations of patriotism and cloaked in the American flag, which turns out to be about as poignant an accessory as a Members Only jacket. *I'm obviously better than you, but why does that creep have one?*

The election did not yield a Kristallnacht exactly. The physical attacks and vandalism spiked briefly postelection, but most of the violence was online; Twitter and subreddits dedicated to Trumpism and the reversal of "white genocide," which is what racist imbeciles call having a black supervisor at work or the intolerable hell of *"para español, marque dos."* Still, the online trolling and doxing were very much the vandalism of the 1938 kind. Triple parentheses ((( ))) on Twitter did double duty, equal parts swastika and Jewish star, declaring ideology and identifying the enemy in six simple keystrokes. White supremacists came out of the woodwork, marching in defense of their "heritage." Assholes in khakis took to the streets of Charlottesville, Virginia, chanting, "Jews will not replace us!"—whatever the hell that is supposed to mean. Then one of them murdered a counter-demonstrator with his car. And then the president of the United States, either because he is a fascist himself or he simply did not wish to antagonize his deplorable base, decided not to point fingers, in a statement that by now has become infamous: "Well, I do think there's blame—yes, I think there's blame on both sides. You look at—you look at both sides. I think there's blame on both sides. And I have no doubt about it, and you don't have any doubt about it either. . . . But you also had people that were very fine people on both sides. . . . You had people in that group that were there to protest the taking down of, to them, a very, very important statue and the renaming of a park from Robert E. Lee to another name."

For what it's worth, just as a bit of historical refresher, Robert E. Lee was the general who led a war against the United States by a secessionist confederacy in defense of enslaving black human beings to get labor costs to be more manageable. That heritage.

But I have no interest in relitigating the Civil War. The point is that the white-identity movement of the right, largely in reaction to the accumulated identity movements of the left, has become an army of virtual brownshirts, parading their hate for all to see and yielding violence that we cannot safely assume will be isolated. In January 2018, it emerged that the accused twenty-year-old in the California murder of a gay, Jewish college student was a member of Atomwaffen Division, a paramilitary neo-Nazi group tied to four killings and dedicated to the overthrow of the mongrelized nation. In October 2018 came the hate-crime murder of two African Americans in a Kentucky Kroger, the mailing of bombs to a dozen figures in the media and on the left, and the murder of twelve Pittsburgh Jews in their synagogue as they worshipped. On August 3, 2019, a white nationalist posted a diatribe of anti-immigrant hatred (what the press widely called, ugh, a "manifesto") on the extremist bulletin board 8chan denouncing Mexican migrants in all the familiar vile ways, in language mirroring the "invasion" rhetoric of Donald Trump. Seventeen minutes later, the same angry white male entered an El Paso Walmart with an AK-47-style assault rifle and started mowing down human beings. Twenty-one were murdered, dozens more injured.

These perpetrators all raged about the enemies of their way of life. What beer they drink and what's on their playlist I do not know.

2

E Pluribus Unum?

The American experiment from the outset was a bit of a paradox: conferring rights on the individual, yes, but for the sake of the common good—no matter how common:

> We the people of the United States, in order to form a more perfect union, establish justice, insure domestic tranquility, provide for the common defence, promote the general welfare, and secure the blessings of liberty to ourselves and our posterity.

Nothing in there about landowners or peerage. From the get-go (pilgrims, Puritans, low-born economic migrants, indentured servants, ex-cons) our national identity was based on heterogeneity, the diverse, highly assimilated whole that was greater than the sum of its parts. The English and the Dutch were followed by the French and the Mexicans and the Germans and the Poles and the Swedes and the Norwegians and the Italians and the Irish and the Serbs and the Chinese and the Jews of Eastern Europe and, since World War II, one hundred and fifty nations and hundreds of ethnicities more. "Give me your tired, your poor, your huddled masses" wasn't a proposal, it was Emma Lazarus's 1883 distillation of the story so far.

The sentiment, after all, was enshrined on the Great Seal of the United States. *E pluribus unum*. It's on our money. It is, literally, our motto—like *Semper Fi* or I'm Lovin' It. President Lincoln liked the analogy of trying to snap an individual stick versus trying the same with a bundle—the second-best metaphor ever for American pluralism. The best, and most enduring, traces to 1782, when French-born American writer J. Hector St. John de Crèvecoeur mused on a unique political and cultural alloy:

> . . . leaving behind him all his ancient prejudices and manners, receives new ones from the new mode of life he has embraced, the government he obeys, and the new rank he holds. He becomes an American by being received in the broad lap of our great Alma Mater. Here individuals of all nations are melted into a new race of men, whose labors and posterity will one day cause great changes in the world.

The melting pot. So ingrained, so central to our self-image is *e pluribus unum* that surely it is immutable.

Isn't it?

If only. History abounds with examples of what seemed immutable no longer being so. Just think about post-WWII Yugoslavia. Catholics married Muslims. Orthodox Serbs worked side by side with Croatian and Slovenian Catholics. But not long after Marshal Tito died, someone decided that certain ethnic groups were getting a raw deal and started paying close attention to the family trees of their neighbors, coworkers, and in-laws. The melting pot became a powder keg. In the Middle East, Gamal Abdel Nassar's dream of pan-Arabism fractured under the strain of tribal, sectarian, and Cold War rivalries. In Rwanda, in the early '90s, culminating in 1994, the majority Hutu government presided over the murder of an estimated one million ethnic Tutsis, eradicating 70 percent of that population though they had shared the real estate for centuries. In the midst of the India/Pakistan partition in 1947, Hindus, Muslims, and Sikhs—though racially of a piece—slaughtered one another by the thousands. In Northern Ireland, Catholics and Protestants warred for the entire twentieth century. And what civilization has not marginalized and/or terrorized Jews since time immemorial? The Holocaust claimed six million Jews. In Germany, the victims had proudly listened to Wagner, read Goethe, been fully integrated into society. And then they died in Dachau. Please take note: Nazi Germany may seem like some distant historical aberration, but humans have walked the earth for 7 million years. Judaism is 3,500 years old. The Holocaust ended only 75 years ago—after the invention of the programmable computer, on the day jazz pianist Keith Jarrett was born. He is still performing.

It was yesterday.

The modern democracies of Europe have spent those 75 years trying to eradicate the conditions, social and political, in which such evil could ever again take root. Truth and reconciliation, laws against Nazism and hate speech, and, perhaps most tellingly, liberal immigration policies. They have welcomed Turks, South Asians, Arabs, and sub-Saharan African migrants with open arms, profiting economically and culturally from diversity while simultaneously constructing a bulwark against toxic nationalism.

They thought. In 2020, the continent is roiled by perceived threats from without, and from within. In the past decade, terrorism, recession, and the Syrian refugee crisis have empowered nationalists and xenophobes from the political fringes ever closer to the mainstream, including parliamentary clout. Meanwhile, separatist movements are active in Denmark, Finland, France, Italy, Lithuania, Moldova, Netherlands, Poland, Romania, Spain, and Switzerland (!). The United Kingdom is *this close* to divorce not only from the European Union, but from Scotland.

Scotland.

Not that ethnic purity is any kind of ideal. Repeatedly in history, homogeneity has been the justification for discrimination and genocide. Imperial Japan was, after all, not a melting pot but an utterly uniform rice pot when it murderously overthrew half of Asia, even as the Germans, in the name of Aryan purity, enslaved Europe.

The headwaters for all these rivers of blood, the universal source of historical catastrophe, is identity. But it does not begin with violence. It begins with talk. Ethnic jokes. Raised eyebrows and tut-tuts. Whispered criticisms, which become slurs, which become accusations, which become propaganda, which become demonization, which become violent episodes, which become genocides.

So watch an evening of *Hannity* and try not to get the chills. Listen to the president of the United States talk about Muslims, Mexicans, Democrats, journalists, judges, NATO allies—or listen to him embrace dictators in Russia, Turkey, Saudi Arabia, the Philippines—and try not to get frightened. Yet in the face of such rhetoric, and government policy in support of it, Americans reflexively respond with unequivocal denial: "But it can't happen here."

Really? That's always seemed to be true. But what if actually the opposite were true? What if our particular history and culture have created an ideal incubation medium for divisiveness? What if America is not only not invulnerable to violent disintegration but predisposed to it? It is a grim exercise, but let us suppose how that might be.

Ponder for a moment that aforementioned paradox: securing the *general* welfare by protecting and empowering the *individual.* Not only are personal rights at the core of our founding documents, so is the pursuit of individual happiness, which was very quickly understood as upward mobility in a classless society. This is not a my-dad-was-a-shepherd-and-his-dad-was-a-shepherd-and-*his*-dad-was-a-shepherd-so-I-suppose-I'll-be-a-shepherd-too sort of nation. Self-actualization is integral to our national story. Just for instance, Abraham Lincoln's mythology—humble beginnings, rough-hewn education, down-to-earth wisdom—predated any actual political accomplishments. From Ragged Dick to Jay Gatsby, our literary archetypes have been self-made men. And we duly revere the real-life exemplars of American pluck. Benjamin Franklin, the Wright brothers, Jobs and Wozniak, Andrew Carnegie, Oprah—the whole pantheon of the vaunted American Dream, as first coined in 1931 by historian James Truslow Adams:

> The American dream that has lured tens of millions of all nations to our shores in the past century has not been a dream of merely material plenty, though that has doubtlessly counted heavily. It has been much more than that. It has been a dream of being able to grow to fullest development as man and woman, unhampered

by the barriers which had slowly been erected in the older civilizations, unrepressed by social orders which had developed for the benefit of classes rather than for the simple human being of any and every class.

What Adams described is less dream than template, a de facto American creed that self-worth derives only from self-improvement. From childhood we are inculcated with the notion that our destiny, our duty, is to transcend our shitty status-quo selves and upgrade. You take a quick audit of who you are, feel appropriately ashamed, then follow the instructions of Thomas Jefferson and your commencement speaker to *be better than that.* The Jeffersonian "pursuit of happiness" was codified in the (federally subsidized) settlement of the West, the beatification of the rugged individualist, and more than a century of popular culture, from Horatio Alger to Dale Carnegie, and from '50s fitness tele-trainer Jack LaLanne to modern makeover reality TV shows: *The Biggest Loser, This Old House, Queer Eye, Desert Car Kings.* This is not to mention the self-help industry, which assumes you are a loser and presumes to remake you into something special, or the zillion or so New Age practices that lure seekers to Santa Fe and Sedona faster than they can build fake adobe condos to house them.

When French diplomat and political scientist Alexis de Tocqueville made his rounds of this country in the 1840s, the universal striving jumped right out at him: "The first thing that strikes a traveler in the United States is the innumerable multitude of those who seek to emerge from their original condition."

And he didn't even see Botox. Unfortunately, human makeovers tend to be the yo-yo diets of self-actualization. Whether your spirit guide is Jenny Craig or Tony Robbins or the Bhagwan Shree Rajneesh, it is only a matter of time before you return to the status quo. One notable case in point would be "the New Nixon." Heavily advertised in 1968 as a changed man (versus his reputation for corruption and paranoia), he turned out to be exactly like the old Nixon, only with an enemies list and more felonies. The acceptance of the New Nixon flew in the face of folk wisdom—"a tiger can't change its stripes"—and at least one popular philosopher, the estimable psychiatric counselor Dr. Lucy van Pelt:

> Lucy: "I think you should work hard to improve your character, Charlie Brown. Once a child gets to be five years old, his character is pretty well established."

> Charlie Brown: "But I'm already five years old! I'm more than five!"

> Lucy: "That's right, you are, aren't you? Too bad, that's the way it goes!"

That advice cost Charlie Brown five cents, but it was a nickel well spent. It is difficult to reinvent yourself, and even more difficult to put a capital *D* on *destiny*. Ben Franklin and Oprah and Michael Bloomberg notwithstanding, the brass ring is elusive. Think about Lennie and George in *Of Mice and Men,* who simply didn't have the wits or wherewithal to acquire property and "live off the fatta the land." Or the crushed spirit of Willy Loman in *Death of a Salesman,* whose narrative of success was a tragic delusion. For every Ragged

Dick, how many Willy Lomans are left disappointed, resentful, and fatally embittered?

This is a subject about which I have more than a casual acquaintance. I spent a dozen years in the late '80s through the '90s in pursuit of the pursuit of happiness, chronicling the exploits of ordinary Americans attempting to achieve their vaunted individual Destinies. They weren't looking for the white picket fence of middle-class stability; they were looking for transformation—hundreds of Americans from all over this map struggling to mold their personas and forge their futures. Like Alphonse Williams, a Bronx bus driver and real-life Ralph Kramden, who bet the rent money on an idea he was certain would change his life. The idea was SpeakEasies, an elasticized disposable paper sleeve for wrapping around pay-phone handsets to prevent the spread of communicable disease.

He couldn't have been expected to imagine a cell phone–dominated near future that would render pay phones obsolete, but you could argue he invested a bit too much faith in folks leaving home with pockets, or pocketbooks, stuffed with phone condoms. Which, needless to add, nobody did. Likewise Jeff Weber, Florida ceiling fan–store manager by day and, by night, owner of Preservation Specialties. He'd bet his $30,000 savings on a contraption that freeze-dried dead pets. Jeff really thought he could knock Big Taxidermy down a peg or two, but for some reason, the freeze-dried-pet category never took off.

I watched eager young couples invest in a racket run by a cheerful con man named Hy Hunter, who charged entrepreneurs $3,000, $5,000, $50,000 a crack to get in on the ground floor of—obviously—worm ranching. He told them that earthworms could naturally turn ordinary garbage into the finest natural fertilizer, which is mostly true. He also told them there was a booming, inexhaustible market for their magic, which was a lie.

"What do you do with heavy metals or materials, you know, that are . . . have been spiced with atoms or hydrogen bombs or something like this?" he posed to me, answering his own question by showing me a handful of worms. "If people will listen to me, we can change the world." The investors listened. The world stayed the same. We are often told to invest in ourselves. We are never told first to read the prospectus.

Consider Garry Waite. He was a Las Vegas endodontist who was certainly well off, but just wasn't satisfied doing root canals; he wanted to be a country music star. He had the guitar and the hat and the silver-tipped cowboy boots. And he had an extremely close relationship with country music legend Tammy Wynette, in the sense that once, in a Vegas hotel dental emergency, he had both hands in her mouth. What he didn't have was an album full of good songs. I actually met him on the occasion of him hanging up his spurs. He'd spent twenty years and $100,000 of his own money trying to achieve his destiny, and wound up like the character in one of his own songs. If stardom was his temptress . . .

. . . "she took my heart, put it on the floor, and stomped that sucker flat."

The reinvention imperative can overtake entire communities. Back when I wrote about Hamilton, Ohio, all it was known for was the old Chem-Dyne plant, a toxic-waste Superfund site that made Love Canal look like Lourdes. The Great Miami River was polluted, and no industrial employers were waiting in the wings. So Hamilton's city fathers decided to make an emphatic restatement of self.

This hard-luck bend in the river ceased to be Hamilton, Ohio. It was rechristened . . .

Hamilton! Ohio.

Yes, they added an exclamation point! No, it didn't work!

These stories were a bit pitiful, a bit noble, a bit hilarious, and more than a bit instructive. All the folks were driven to unhappiness by the pursuit of happiness, the unspoken corollary of which is, nobody stays happy forever selling ceiling fans for someone else. No, once again, we are inculcated from birth with the notion that self-worth derives from self-improvement . . . and we attach a reciprocal sense of failure in this Land of Opportunity to the mere status quo. The instructive bit: Our supposed birthright is setting us up to fail.

Visualize Jeff Weber's empty freeze-dryer and broaden that picture several millionfold. Think about the disappointment, and the embarrassment, and the umbrage that goes with the fear that you've been sold a bill of goods. Because there's a lot of that going around. Indeed, as economic historian Rutger Bregman writes in *Utopia for Realists*, "Frankly, there's almost no country on Earth where the American Dream is less likely to come true than in the U.S. of A. Anybody eager to work their way up from rags to riches is better off trying their luck in Sweden, where people born into poverty can still hold out hope of a brighter future."

The sense of shaky financial footing, especially in rural America and the Rust Belt, has been well documented, notably by researcher Tess Wise of Harvard's Department of Government in her study *Economic Insecurity and American Political Culture* and the London School of Economics professor Michael McQuarrie in "The Revolt of the Rust Belt: Place and Politics in the Age of Anger." Without understating the role of cultural backlash and naked racism, there is no ignoring the fact that millions of Americans feel—or, at least, *say* that they feel—nervous about their financial circumstances. And many of these people have found a champion, someone unafraid to put his mouth where their money isn't.

From July 2015 to August 2016, the Gallup organization surveyed 112,995 American adults about their sense of economic security. In response to the question "Are you feeling better about your financial situation these days, or not?" Trump supporters answered no 23 percentage points more than those disapproving of him. As Gallup's Jonathan Rothwell wrote, "The financial insecurity gap between those who do and do not view Trump favorably cannot be explained by income or other objective economic and social circumstances. The relationship between viewing Trump favorably and feeling financially insecure holds even after statistically controlling for individual factors such as age, veteran status, gender, race, ethnicity, employment status, education, occupational category, religion, party affiliation, and ideology."

This despite a booming economy and low unemployment, as the effects of the 2008 financial crisis and the ensuing Great Recession had gradually subsided. When Trump took office, median household incomes had risen for two straight years, and so had consumer spending, perhaps a more accurate representation of financial mood than survey responses. But those are statistics, which do not have dominion over our feelings or our fears.

The reminders were everywhere, after all, that globalization and automation had taken their toll. Hundreds of thousands of high-wage manufacturing jobs had been lost to overseas labor markets and domestic robots. Real wages—that is, adjusted for inflation—for adult non-farm labor at the median level of earnings had increased only 6.1 percent over twenty-seven years. And among men at that median earnings level, real wages had *decreased* 6 percent.

Meantime, healthcare insurance was chewing up ever-larger chunks of household income. Land of Opportunity, land of *schmopportunity*; the Silicon Valley billionaires and the bankers and the rest of the elite 1 percent were enjoying greater and greater shares of the pie, and the rest of us were fighting over crumbs. The majority of working-class Americans were doing no better than running in place, and many significantly worse than that. Oh, and the Census Bureau reminds us that in 2045 whites will cease to be a majority.

Then what will be taken away?

If American identity hinges on somehow or another getting ahead, give some thought to the agony of losing ground. How are you supposed to pursue happiness, to be a better version of yourself, when powerful forces are aligned to piss on who you are to begin with? Does our current crisis force us to reckon with the collateral damage of the American Dream? Has America broken its founding promise?

To answer that question rationally requires some soul-searching. To *feel* the answer is another matter. Viscera are handy that way. In so many places and in so many ways, the society is hemorrhaging hope. And, naturally, opportunists smell the blood. Conservative politicians and right-wing media wage the culture wars 24/7. Obama was a tyrant. Feminazis and the Gillette razor brand are emasculating you. Sharia law is coming to your town. Welfare queens are ripping you off. Transgender freaks will molest your children in the restroom. Bureaucrats are subverting elected officials. Mexican rapists and drug dealers are surging over the border. Our country is surrendering our sovereignty to the UN. The Jews and the schools and the media and the department stores and the devil of secular humanism have declared war on Christmas! Has the American promise been broken? Yes! The elites are making fools of you. Are you just going to stand there and take it?

None of these accusations has even the slightest basis in fact; they are quintessential examples of scapegoating, the menacing drumbeat of propagandists and demagogues. Yet for vast swaths of the electorate, they are perceived as courageous truth telling. Why? Part of the reason, as we shall closely examine in the next chapter, is that much of America has been conditioned for decades to subscribe to such a narrative. Another reason is simple human nature. As anthropologists, historians, and psychologists well understand, we are not only equipped but programmed to assign blame, to identify "us" versus some sinister, culpable "them." All we have to do, for the instinct to be triggered, is to perceive a threat to the group with which we identify. In a 2018 *On the Media* conversation, professor Lilliana Mason of the University of Maryland told me

> the most powerful identities are the ones whose status is being threatened. . . . and it's very easy to make people think about one identity or another simply by telling them that someone has insulted their group or that their group is about to lose in some type of competition. When we see politicians talking about identities or groups, one thing that they have a lot of power in is helping us think about which groups are most important to us by telling us which groups are the most threatened.

Mason, the author of *Uncivil Agreement: How Politics Became Our Identity*, cited a watershed psychological experiment dramatizing the ease of such manipulation. Undertaken in 1954 by University of Oklahoma psychologist Muzafer Sherif, it was a study on

"inter-group relations" and has come to be known as the Robbers
Cave Experiment.

About two dozen twelve-year-olds of white working-class
backgrounds—chosen for good physical and emotional health—
were bused to a Boy Scout camp in Robbers Cave State Park and divided into two groups. Each group was aware of, though segregated
from, the other. In the first week, the researchers (playing the role
of counselors) organized activities for each group that required cooperation among them, but not with the boys from the other group.
Sure enough, each group forged an image of itself vis-à-vis the other.
One, without prompting, dubbed itself the Rattlers. The other likewise called itself the Eagles. After six days in the woods, they had
become tribes and not only encouraged the counselors to arrange
competitions between them but voiced annoyance about privileges
and camp resources each tribe deemed to be disproportionately favoring their rivals.

The counselors then amplified the rivalry by offering prizes, like
cash or penknives, to the winners of the various contests, and zip to
the losers, whereupon both groups became increasingly chauvinistic
and territorial. They hoisted team flags, insulted one another in the
dining hall, sang songs ridiculing the other group, and—when they
feared their turf was going to be violated—threatened violence. This
state of agitated Otherness required all of two weeks to develop.
Some Eagles and Rattlers demanded that meals be staggered so they
would not have to dine together.

That was the Robbers Cave Experiment. Now I will tell you
about the Market Street Experiment. This was me, in an Uber
headed a mile west from Center City Philadelphia to the University
of Pennsylvania. Philadelphia is on the other side of the Delaware

River from Camden, New Jersey, and it so happened that a car with Jersey tags cut off our car at an intersection.

"Can you believe these people," my driver said. "Look at them. They think they can come over here and do this shit. They don't know how to drive. They don't know how to behave. Why don't they just stay where they belong. Those people make me sick."

It doesn't take long, and it doesn't take much, to despise an Other. In fact, sometimes it's even me. Here's a nice little note I got recently:

> Garfield, YOU are a left wing horse's ass. You are CLUELESS and your hatred of Trump is irrational. Clinton was CORRUPT— that's both Bill AND Hillary. The idiot gay African was and is evil. He stacked EVERY agency with his America hating jackasses. You have ZERO credibility your bearded fool. What are you going to do when you leftists start another civil war? Keep it up and it WILL occur.

Civil war? Not very *e pluribus unum*–y. Also, shouldn't "America hating" be hyphenated?

3

But of Course Trumpism

How do you not remember where you were that day? January 20, 2017. For brand-new presidential press secretary Sean Spicer, the memory was indelible. "This was the largest audience to ever witness an inauguration—period—both in person and around the globe." Never mind the aerial photos, which told a different story, it was probably a crowd in the 12 to 16 trillion range crammed into the National Mall from the Capitol past the Lincoln Memorial to South Carolina and beyond, all the way to Antarctica and then Jupiter. Not only bigger than Obama's, but probably the largest gathering of earthlings in the history of time. Then, suddenly, the new president approached the lectern for his inaugural speech, and a light rain began to fall. Dignitaries on the dais fumbled with ponchos. Somewhere in the U.K., an actress with the magnificent name Clíodhna McCorley was watching on TV and fumbled for her smartphone. "That's not

rain at Trump's #Inauguration," she tweeted, "that's God's tears."
Touché, Clíodhna.

Now, the thing about weather—much like a crowd—is it forms
in front of eyewitnesses. And it also happens to be very meticulously
recorded. Plus, in this case, televised live around the world. So naturally, forty-five hours later, Trump lied about it.

"The truth is," Donald J. Trump declared, "it stopped immediately, and then became sunny. And I walked off, and it poured after
I left. It poured."

One of the very first of many thousands—*thousands*—of lies
documented during his presidency. But if we are interested in metaphor, yes, it has poured. It has been a fucking deluge. I certainly remember where I was that day: on my sofa, still incredulous, thinking
bad thoughts about the Electoral College. The phrase that popped
into my head was: "You broke it; you bought it."

Yes, America is a damaged democracy overseen by a damaged
boy-man. Our society has surely "had a great fall." But it's not as
though the cracks developed overnight. The fissures and fractures
have been decades in the making, in direct parallel to that frightening phenomenon called "change." For sixty years, court decisions and
legislation have fleshed out the Bill of Rights to offer all Americans
equal protection under the law, more or less in synchrony with the
liberal democracies of Europe. Miranda warnings. Prayer in schools.
Desegregation. *Roe v. Wade.* Affirmative action. Gays in the military. Same-sex marriages. The gender spectrum. Not to mention gun
control, sex education, and the teaching of evolution. And also not
to mention female pastors, female soldiers, female bosses, and—is
nothing sacred?—female play-by-play announcers. To a significant
chunk of the population, it was as if the atheists and the race-card
players and the sodomites and the feminazis had won. If things kept

heading in that direction, we were going to wind up with a black president sitting in the White House.

Whether you were thrilled or disgusted by these watersheds, they were so globally viewed as social progress that in 1991 political scientist Francis Fukuyama declared *The End of History*, the final chapter in a worldwide consensus of government responsibilities and human rights. To Fukuyama, who documented the embrace of social justice reforms and respect for civil rights even in hitherto "backward" societies on every continent, the trajectory toward universal liberal democracy was unstoppable. Maybe a little tidying up to be done in Somalia and North Korea, but basically: game over. It was a squeaker for a millennium or so, but Enlightenment had ended up running the table.

Alas, to paraphrase Mark Twain, reports of the death of history have been greatly exaggerated.

Turns out that each of these incremental civic protections was viewed by large swaths of the population not as a safeguard but as a slap in the face, an assault on their "traditional values," and, consequently, a repudiation by the liberal elites of their very selves. This did not sit well, and so commenced the culture wars, waged by conservatives over perceived lost primacy in a country they less and less recognized. As Moral Majority cofounder the Rev. Jerry Falwell put it in announcing his Holy War against the infidels, "Americans have literally stood by and watched as godless, spineless leaders have brought our nation floundering to the brink of death."

Does that language sound familiar? A generation earlier, the culture wars were foreshadowed by McCarthyism, a dark period of the early 1950s when government officials, prominent private-sector leaders, celebrities, and ordinary citizens stood accused of disloyalty to America, and the rest of the body politic stood accused of suicidal complacency in the midst of the Red Scare. The pretext was supposed Communist infiltration of the society; the effect was a reign of terror that did not end until the national repudiation of demagogic Sen. Joseph McCarthy. In the meantime, the nation was riven by fear and mistrust, breaking down along similar ideological lines—owing partly, yes, to actual left-wing activism by American salon Communists in the '30s and '40s, when the brutality and moral bankruptcy of Soviet Communism was obscured by utopian propaganda about social justice.

The crisis faded, but ideological battle lines soon reemerged, when in 1967 presidential candidate Richard Nixon—who cut his political teeth as an inquisitor on the House Un-American Activities Committee—found a domestic bogeyman to substitute for the Russians, namely the liberal elites. As *New York Post* columnist Pete Hamill wrote, "he practiced the policies of resentment as it had never been practiced before on a national stage; cultivating the haters, the resenters, the paranoids, he played on the very worst instincts of Americans on his way to power, and when he finally attained power, he did not change." Hamill harbored some guilt over what he was witnessing, because it was his 1969 article for *New York Magazine*, "The Revolt of the Lower Middle Class," that is said to have inspired Nixon into building his party's 1970 midterm campaigns on a foundation of white resentment.

Nixon's so-called Southern Strategy successfully pried away conservative white Dixiecrats, who bridled at the Democratic Party's perceived hostility toward religion and its explicit hostility to entrenched racism. First they voted for Nixon, then they registered Republican. The Civil Rights Act, signed by Lyndon B. Johnson, might as well have been called the Say So Long to Mississippi, Alabama, Georgia, Arkansas, North Carolina, South Carolina, Kentucky, and

Louisiana Act. To this day, they are the reddest of red states. The Crimson Tide, you might say. And to this day, the Republican Party owes its legislative dominance (31–19 even after the so-called Blue Wave of the 2018 midterm elections) to rural white voters smoldering with resentment about liberal overreach. Indeed, there was no risk of those embers ever dying because there would be no shortage of interested parties pumping bellows, especially from Christian conservative activists.

Further intervention by the federal government, from school busing to *Roe v. Wade*, led to the broad national movement dubbed the religious right. From the late '70s, such groups as Christian Voice, the Religious Roundtable Council, the Christian Coalition, Focus on the Family, the Family Research Council, and the American Family Association coalesced to form an imposing and dependable voting bloc, credited with propelling Ronald Reagan, George H. W. Bush, George W. Bush, and even (astonishingly) the morally vacuous Donald Trump into the White House. For the past thirty years, every candidate for the Republican presidential nomination has been obliged to make the pilgrimage to Liberty University (previously Liberty Baptist College) in Lynchburg, Virginia, the rural redoubt of the redoubtable (late) Jerry Falwell. He wasn't necessarily a kingmaker, but every primary season he was a potential kingbreaker. So if you sought the Republican nomination for a national office, you were obliged to hit the campaign trail singing his tune. And what tune? This from his 1980 book, *Listen America:*

> We must reverse the trend America finds herself in today. Young people between the ages of twenty-five and forty have been born and reared in a different world than Americans of years past. The television set has been their primary baby-sitter. From the

television set they have learned situation ethics and immorality—they have learned a loss of respect for human life. They have learned to disrespect the family as God has established it. They have been educated in a public-school system that is permeated with secular humanism. . . .

The hope of reversing the trends of decay in our republic now lies with the Christian public in America. We cannot expect help from the liberals. They certainly are not going to call our nation back to righteousness and neither are the pornographers, the smut peddlers, and those who are corrupting our youth.

Note the reference to "secular humanism." This was the catchall term embraced by Falwell and his cofounder Tim LaHaye to literally demonize the many manifestations of liberal activism in order to (as they so often preached) deliver America from the grip of Satan.

Secular humanism is, of course, a thing; as an outlook on the world, it defines ethics and morality not as biblical dogma or a dictate from a supreme being, but a function of human reason, wisdom, empathy, and conscience. Now, reason and empathy aren't in and of themselves controversial—unless someone under the influence of hubris or Satan presumes them to be a substitute or, worse yet, opposition to the word of God. Then you've got trouble. That notion of dangerous irreligiosity is just what evangelical theologian Francis Schaeffer complained about in the early 1970s, and the complaint resonated. By the time Falwell began to preach against it, secular humanism had already been characterized as an organized, agenda-driven conspiracy to undermine Christianity and American values. This from the June 1980 edition of *Christian Harvest Times* magazine: "To understand humanism is to understand women's liberation, the ERA, gay rights, children's rights, abortion, sexual education, the 'new' morality, evolution, values clarification, situational ethics, the separation of church and state, the loss of patriotism, and many of the other problems that are tearing America apart today." Plus, I think, fibromyalgia, gasoline prices, and airplane food. Because the Godless humanists were everywhere.

A year earlier, an Oregon radio preacher named Leo Wine became a minor cause célèbre after airing a series of broadcasts that channeled Joe McCarthy, with just a touch of General Jack D. Ripper from *Dr. Strangelove*:

> Humanist obsessions: sex, pornography, marijuana, drugs, self-indulgence, rights without responsibility....
>
> Now the humanist organizations . . . control the television, the radio, the newspapers, the Hollywood movies, magazines, porno magazines, and the unions, the Ford Foundation, Rockefeller Foundation. . . . They have infiltrated until every department of our country is controlled by the humanists.
>
> . . . the humanists hope to name their own dictator who will create out of the ashes of our pro-moral republic a humanist Utopia, an atheistic, socialistic, amoral humanist society for America and the rest of the world. In fact, their goal is to accomplish that takeover by or before the year 2000.

That, again, was from the olden times of forty years ago. Wine's ravings came to national attention only because of a complaint filed against him under the now-defunct fairness doctrine, which had mandated equal broadcast time for objections to controversial views espoused over the airwaves. There was no internet, or Fox News Channel, or even a national Rush Limbaugh radio show to spread the word of imminent destruction of our way of life. But such nightmare scenarios did resonate nonetheless, and were already being seized upon by politicians whose ears are kept to the ground for precisely such vibrations of discontent.

In 1976, U.S. Rep. John Conlan (R-Arizona) introduced an amendment to the year's education bill that would prohibit federal funding in support of secular humanism. The amendment failed. But in 1984, Sen. Orrin Hatch (R-Utah) succeeded in passing just such a provision. (It eventually expired under the underlying legislation's sunset provisions, apparently without ever having been invoked to kill funding.) School boards around the country took the ball and ran with it, censoring textbooks and supplemental reading they deemed to advance secular humanist goals. In some jurisdictions, creationism (rebranded "intelligent design") was mandated to be taught alongside Darwin.

This had echoes of the so-called Scopes Monkey Trial of 1925, in which a substitute high school teacher was prosecuted for violation of Tennessee's new Butler Act prohibiting the teaching of evolution. It was the show trial of the decade, and the show ended in a conviction. The verdict was later reversed on a technicality, but the battle between religion and science—another distant foreshadowing of today's catastrophic polarization—did not end there. Nor did it end with the landmark 1968 Supreme Court decision *Epperson v. Arkansas* prohibiting the prohibition against teaching evolution. Why would it, any more than the Civil War ended at Appomattox Court House? A 2017 MSN poll found that 87 percent of Republicans oppose removal of Confederate statues from public spaces, and a 2017 Gallup poll found that that 38 percent of Americans believe that the world was created by God in six days within the past ten thousand years.

On the subject of the Civil War, by the way, rationalized then and now as a righteous struggle for the sovereignty of individual states against the meddling of an overzealous national government, the invocation of states' rights against intrusive Big Government continues to be an evergreen trope in dividing the put-upon "us" from the tyrannical "them." If you ever hear a politician talk about Big Government, there are two things of which you can be sure:

1. He is trying to piss off his base.
2. His *Republican* base.

That's where the Tea Party movement came from. A decade ago, this hard-right faction of the Republican Party framed the movement as the American Revolution Redux, the heroic struggle of patriots against the tyrant Barack Obama and his elitist accomplices conspiring to deprive Americans of their liberty. As U.S. Rep. Michele Bachmann (R-Minnesota) told the Western Conservative Summit in 2010, "We will talk a little bit about what has transpired in the last eighteen months . . . turning our country into a nation of slaves."

Big Government. Confederate flags. Evolution. These are what are called "wedge issues." Politicians use the sledgehammers of legislation and rhetoric, and interest groups use the sledgehammers of campaign contributions and litigation, to drive in the wedges. Even when they know all they'll gain is popular support. In the case of creationism versus evolution, for instance, over the past forty years, federal courts have repeatedly been obliged to cite the Establishment Clause of the First Amendment to keep religious doctrine out of the classroom. This includes notable cases in California (1981), Arkansas (1982), Louisiana (1987), Illinois (1990), California (1994), Louisiana (1997), Minnesota (2000), and Pennsylvania (2005). The outcomes were foregone conclusions; this is settled law. But the votes and donations keep coming in, and the emotions create a chilling effect that to some degree serves their ideological interests. The 2008 survey of National Association of Biology Teachers found that 20 percent of its membership feels pressure to deemphasize evolution in their classrooms. Meantime, Darwin v. Genesis, like *Roe v. Wade* and North v. South and Coke v. Pepsi, is a perpetual war.

Another is school prayer. In two Kennedy administration–era decisions—*Engel v. Vitale* on June 25, 1962, and *Abington School District v. Schempp* on June 17, 1963—the Supreme Court cited the Establishment Clause to declare school-sponsored prayer and Bible readings unconstitutional. Once again, this was as settled as any court precedent can be, constantly argued in the federal courts and constantly affirmed, because the founders were so explicit: "Congress shall make no law respecting an establishment of religion, or prohibiting the free exercise thereof." Court after court has found that sanctioning Christian prayer in government facilities, or any other religion's prayer for the matter, is tantamount to embracing that religion.

To many on the Christian right, this doctrine is something akin to liberalism's original sin, and they have been fighting it for fifty-six years, sometimes by arguing that the Christian founders absolutely believed the law should reflect their religious beliefs, sometimes by arguing that honoring Christian values isn't the same as establishing an official religion, and sometimes simply by arguing that prayer-free schools are the root of most evil.

In April 2018, for instance, Kansas legislator and Tea Party Republican Randy Garber offered the answer for sexually transmitted infections, out-of-wedlock births, and, duh, SAT scores: "I say the way to fix our schools," he said, "is to put prayer and the Bible back in and give it a chance."

The previous February, Steve Lonegan, unsuccessful Tea Party candidate for the Republican nomination in New Jersey's fifth congressional district, said moral deterioration in the post–school prayer environment is resulting in mass shootings: "It's just so disturbing that society has deteriorated to this point morally that we're confronted with this. And if there's ever a time to return prayer to the classroom, now's the time."

And then there was the Lafayette, Louisiana, school board, which on November 11, 2001, found the antidote for terrorism. Here are the last three of its twelve *whereas*es:

WHEREAS, no power to prescribe any religious exercise, or to assume authority in religious discipline, has been delegated to the general government, it must then rest with the States, as far as it can be in any human authority (Thomas Jefferson); and,

WHEREAS, one day every valley shall be exalted and every hill and mountain shall be made low, the rough place will be made plain and the crooked places will be made straight, and the glory of the Lord shall be revealed, and all flesh shall see it together; this is our hope; this is the faith (Martin Luther King, Jr.); and,

WHEREAS, after the terrible tragedies of September 11, 2001, our nation needs the power of prayer perhaps as never before; now,

THEREFORE, BE IT RESOLVED, that the Lafayette Parish School Board calls upon all our federal officials to reconsider the restrictions placed upon the public expression of religious faith in the form of spoken prayer and allow all faiths to express their beliefs in the form of public, spoken prayer.

But here's the thing about the evangelical movement: It failed. Failed to undo the Establishment Clause, failed to overturn *Roe v. Wade*, failed to resist the juggernaut of liberal democracy, failed to rally "values-based voters" in sufficient numbers to overcome the demographics of a changing nation. It waged the culture wars for decades . . . but at least so far has lost. I can't quite say the apotheosis of their futility was the acceptance of transgender Americans in the armed forces, but there are those who saw that as unthinkable. Among them, Tony Perkins of the Christian right pillar, the Family Research Council: "The social extremism that characterized the last eight [Obama] years still haunts the Defense Department at a time when the military can least afford it," Perkins declared. "With ISIS torching its way across the Middle East, our troops shouldn't be torn between its role securing America and securing the Left's radical social agenda. . . . The [new Trump] administration needs to decide: does it want an army of cultural guinea pigs or a lethal force defending America?"

Trump, naturally, promptly reversed Obama's order, but so far has been stymied by a federal court on discrimination grounds.

And therein lies the point. Constantly being stymied by the system, constant repudiation, constant failure yields constant frustration. And often enough frustration yields rage.

Not just from evangelical Christians, but from wide swaths of white culture, feeling humiliated by social justice movements, feminists, immigrants, the media, blacks, Jews, and other perceived threats to their way of life, not least of which the so-called political correctness that they saw invading their churches, their sports, their late-night TV, and their places of employment. Want to make a working man angry? Inform him that the joke he just told is inappropriate. Then put that in his personnel file. Then make him go to a seminar. He doesn't like your sanctimony, and he doesn't want HR—or some justice warrior—telling him what to do. Here's Jack Cashill of WND, a fundamentalist Christian conspiracy theorist site, on that very subject: "Progressives add new sins regularly and new sinners daily. An awkward phrase, a misunderstood joke, a manufactured quote, a frank look at data, a persistent belief in a revered tradition can cost you your job."

The tyranny of the left, in other words. Floundering amid a sense of lost cultural and economic dominance, a loose Coalition of the Unwilling has flipped the script to embrace grievance and victimhood themselves, rediscovering their identity in that very rage. Meet the alt-right, where the law of unintended consequences meets the mentality of resentment and provides a soft target for demagoguery.

Actually, let's *not* meet the entire alt-right, which is less a cohesive movement than a confederation of grievance, sort of the United Way of anger. We can momentarily dispense with the white nationalists, the white supremacists, the Holocaust deniers, the skinheads, the Klansmen, the Islamophobes, and xenophobic hate groups. American Vanguard, Identity Evropa, National Policy Institute, New Century Foundation, Traditionalist Worker Party, National Alliance, National Socialist Movement, American Freedom Party, Aryan Strikeforce, ACT for America—these are just various flavors of neo-Nazis, fueled by hate for blacks, Hispanics, Muslims, and Jews. According to the Southern Poverty Law Center, their organizations are growing rapidly, but they are in the traditional hate business. In the darkest days of the culture wars, there is nothing especially remarkable about their resurgence. As Chris Rock says in his stand-up, "That train's never late." No, what's remarkable about the alt-right coalition is the nature of the other trains.

One of them is the Christian right, the most radical elements of which—chiefly the Christian Patriot and Christian Identity movements—overlap with the fascist ambitions of the white nationalists. This is somewhat bizarre, because to the degree that the alt-right has any coherent ideology, it is atheistic—even pagan—and often explicitly hostile to Christianity. Certainly the central racism of white supremacy, white nationalism, and so on is incompatible with scripture and Christian love—as angrily declared by the Southern Baptist Convention in the immediate wake of Charlottesville, resolving to "decry every form of racism, including alt-right white supremacy, as antithetical to the Gospel of Jesus Christ." Indeed, the pantheon of Christian denominations issued similarly forceful rebukes. But these declarations elided over some very treacherous common ground: namely, continual claims from their own pulpits of victimization and marginalization at the hands of society.

"For more than fifty years, there has been a cultural narrative about the global persecution of Christians that has infused a great deal of evangelical culture and activism," writes Melani McAlister, associate professor of American studies and international affairs at George Washington University and author of *The Kingdom of God Has No Borders: A Global History of American Evangelicals.*

> This . . . has a number of effects. It certainly has increased support for Christian communities that are facing violence or threats in the Middle East and Africa. . . . But it also has the effect of helping Americans to identify themselves, as Christians, as part of a globally oppressed or marginalized group. Thus, we can arrive at the shocking reality that, in 2017, 57 percent of white U.S. evangelicals told pollsters that they believe American Christians face a great deal of discrimination today, while only 44 percent said

the same was true of Muslims. That is, the idea of Christians as victims on the international stage encourages a sense of aggrieved marginality among white American evangelicals. . . . The alt-right can count on people to find something compelling in narratives of their own victimization.

That's not just academic blather from the ivory tower. Her notion is seconded by Greg Johnson, the author of the explicitly racist *White Nationalist Manifesto*, who sees militant Christians as useful idiots in the cause of a white state. "Christian White Nationalists," he proposed, "should be recruited as a fifth column to sow division in the churches, simultaneously weakening their ability to support multiculturalism and preparing for eventual White Nationalist hegemony over them."

Writing for the Christian Research Institute, journalist Richard Abanes sees Johnson getting his wish: "Christians are especially susceptible to the conspiracy theories circulating in patriot/militia circles because they fit nicely into premillennialism, which is currently the most popular evangelical eschatology. Pivotal to this last-days scenario is the idea that just before the world's end a final period of unparalleled turmoil—the Tribulation—will occur under a satanic dictator, the Antichrist."

Now, if that seems far-fetched—imputing a shared sense of victimization on the religious and alt-rights—permit me to reintroduce you to the transitive property of math. A = B and B = C, so A = C. The *B* in this analogy is Donald Trump. He was the darling of the alt-right in the 2016 election, and he was beneficiary of 81 percent of the evangelical vote. Trump ran a campaign of slander against Mexicans and Muslims (and many others). He dog-whistled constantly about "globalists" and "cosmopolitans." He was a shameless adulterer and serial false witness. He called for the jailing of his political opponents. He insulted war heroes and a Gold Star family. He was caught on tape gloating about sexual assault. In all, pretty much the antithesis of the Gospel of Jesus Christ. Strange that *he* was not universally rebuked by the pantheon of denominations. On the contrary, he was embraced, praised, and elected. And yet, six months later, the Southern Baptist Convention was shocked, shocked that there was racism going on in Virginia.

The hear-no-evil, see-no-evil effect is sometimes jaw-dropping. The Liberty Counsel ("We believe every person is created in the image of God and should be treated with dignity and respect. We believe that discourse should be civil and respectful. We condemn violence and hatred and do not support any person or group that advocates or promotes violence or hate.") is a Southern Baptist "ministry" that ministers mainly by suing governments over matters of abortion, Christian religious "freedom," and "family values." Yet it seems ready for Trump, who treats the Ten Commandments like a bucket list to be carved onto Mount Rushmore. "In one and a half years," writes chairman Mat Staver, "Donald Trump and his policies have done more to advance life, religious liberty, the economy, deregulation, government reform, and Israel in the history of America. More pro-life and pro-religious liberty policies have been implemented in this short time than all previous presidents combined. It is no wonder certain segments of the media would rather focus on a negative narrative than these accomplishments."

The Family Research Council is a much bigger player in evangelical politics, but no less prepared to ignore illegal hush-money payoffs to porn stars as long as its political interests are satisfied. In January 2018, FRC president Tony Perkins told podcaster

Edward-Isaac Dovere, "We kind of gave him—'All right, you get a mulligan. You get a do-over here.'"

And why turn a blind eye to conduct that mocks the most fundamental principles of so-called values voters? Oh, because the highly moral faithful "were tired of being kicked around by Barack Obama and his leftists. And I think they are finally glad that there's somebody on the playground that is willing to punch the bully." Perkins means bullies like Gold Star families, federal judges, Vietnam war heroes, sexually abused women, and desperate migrant families. Not bullies like "fine" Nazi protesters, or dictators like Vladimir Putin, Recep Erdogan, and Rodrigo Duterte, who jail and kill people with impunity.

Evangelist Franklin Graham is another who thinks it's a good bargain: "We certainly don't hold him up as the pastor of this country, and he's not," he said on MSNBC. "But I appreciate the fact that the president does have a concern for Christian values, he does have a concern to protect Christians—whether it's here at home or around the world—and I appreciate the fact that he protects religious liberty and freedom."

Religious freedom? The Muslims and "globalists" might see that a slightly different way. But the exclusion of inconvenient truths is a fact of political life, even evangelical-political life. If the birth of the religious right can be traced to Jerry Falwell's demonization of liberalism, now—courtesy of his son and heir to the presidency of Liberty University, Jerry Falwell Jr.—comes acknowledgment of hear-no-evil on a breathtaking scale. In an eye-opening interview with *The Washington Post* early in 2019 came this exchange:

WP: Is there anything President Trump could do that would endanger that support from you or other evangelical leaders?

Falwell: No.

WP: That's the shortest answer we've had so far.

Falwell: Only because I know that he only wants what's best for this country, and I know anything he does, it may not be ideologically "conservative," but it's going to be what's best for this country, and I can't imagine him doing anything that's not good for the country.

WP: Is it hypocritical for evangelical leaders to support a leader who has advocated violence and who has committed adultery and lies often? I understand that a person can be forgiven their sins, but should that person be leading the country?

Falwell: When Jesus said we're all sinners, he really meant all of us, everybody. I don't think you can choose a president based on their personal behavior because even if you choose the one that you think is the most decent—let's say you decide Mitt Romney. Nobody could be a more decent human being, better family man. But there might be things that he's done that we just don't know about. So you don't choose a president based on how good they are; you choose a president based on what their policies are. That's why I don't think it's hypocritical.

There's two kingdoms. There's the earthly kingdom and the heavenly kingdom. In the heavenly kingdom the responsibility is to treat others as you'd like to be treated. In the earthly kingdom, the responsibility is to choose leaders who will do what's best for your country. Think about it. Why have Americans been able to do more to help people in need around the world than any other country in history? It's because of free enterprise, freedom, ingenuity, entrepreneurism and wealth. A poor person never gave anyone a job. A poor person never gave anybody charity, not of any real volume. It's just common sense to me.

Call it moral-majority relativism. What would Jesus do? Well, for evangelicals *not* to support Donald J. Trump, Falwell Jr. said, "may be immoral."

Whatever the degree of common cause among Christians, Trumpistas, and actual Nazis, the Christians were relative latecomers to the party. The "alternative right" as a vague umbrella for various white-nationalist groups had been floated around 2010 but never got much traction. What gave the alt-right its critical mass, its energy, and many of its malicious tactics was a bunch of irritable, militant, misogynistic . . . video gamers.

It began in 2013, when game designer Zoe Quinn released *Depression Quest,* which had no guns or mayhem or hot babes in tight clothing or any of the violent staples of mainstream gaming. It didn't even have pictures; it was an entirely text-based—and somewhat autobiographical—exploration of depression. So naturally male gamers began to harass Quinn for so arrogantly "politicizing" sacrosanct gaming culture and not piling up enough dead warriors. This took the form of thousands of rape threats, beating threats, death threats, and the solicitation of more malicious behavior through the info-vandalism known as doxing. The supposed scandal, and ensuing reign of online terror, was dubbed Gamergate.

"The Internet spent the last month spreading my personal information around," Quinn wrote, "sending me threats, hacking anyone suspected of being friends with me, calling my dad and telling him

I'm a whore, sending nude photos of me to colleagues, and basically giving me the 'burn the witch' treatment."

And the same treatment was visited upon those who defended her, all orchestrated through a lattice of anarchic message boards like 4chan and 8chan, Twitter accounts, and various subreddits with such hacker sophistication that police were never able to track down the culprits. It was, in short, a mob. But the mob became a confederacy, glomming on to various elements of the so-called manosphere and the men's rights movement, from predatory "pick-up artists" who follow the *Return of Kings* and *Chateau Heartiste* blogs to antifeminist ideologues who believe men have been systematically emasculated to the diaspora of disdain for "social justice warriors"—a term of non-endearment for progressives of every stripe, but mainly those who advocate for women. About 260,000 of them congregated on the Red Pill subreddit, which particularly specializes in what to do when you've been accused of date rape, until it was shut down in September 2018. The founder of the Red Pill wrote that it is "evolutionarily advantageous" for a forty-year-old man to proposition a fifteen-year-old girl. In 2013 he wrote, "I treat women like they're subordinate creatures, and suddenly they respect me." And, later, "every woman wants to be attractive enough to be raped." In April 2017, the *Daily Beast* was able to discover his identity. He is Robert Fisher, who at the time was a two-term Republican member of the New Hampshire House of Representatives and vocal proponent of family values. Now he is a former member of the New Hampshire House of Representatives.

Some of these haunts attempt to put an intellectual, anthropological, or evolutionary gloss on their ideology, but in this universe, women are sluts and "basic bitches" and worse. And one of their most prominent voices, the blogger Roosh V, has written at length about his sympathy for the Naziest Nazis of the alt-right. After attending a contentious meeting of the benignly named white-supremacist National Policy Institute, he even wrote a nice shout-out to its founder. (Unless I've missed something and don't understand the meaning of the headline "I Do Not Disavow Richard Spencer.") These are your stars of the manosphere.

And among them, the most remarkable subset, the ultimate expression of grievance identity. They are called "incels." For "involuntarily celibate." They would, if they could, be pick-up artists, but for some reason the sluts and basic bitches don't want any part of them. And of course it is women's fault.

Now it is true, and has always been true, that some males have difficulty attracting women. Maybe because of their looks, or because they are isolated, or because they're crippled by shyness or fear of rejection, or because their teeth are rotting and they stink to high heaven, or because they are dull. Or awkward. Or obnoxious. Or mean. Or perpetually drunk. Or mentally ill. Or just somehow creepy. This lonely cohort has always existed and, with varying degrees of pity and scorn, been categorized as sad sacks. What they never were, until very recently, was a movement of self-declared victims, some of them roiling in unspeakable rage.

On April 23, 2014, a Santa Barbara City College dropout named Elliot Rodger posted a video on YouTube. He titled it "Elliot Rodger's Retribution." Here is some of what he had to say:

I'm twenty-two years old and I'm still a virgin. I've never even kissed a girl. I've been through college for two and a half years, more than that actually, and I'm still a virgin. It has been very torturous. College is the time when everyone experiences those things such as sex and fun and pleasure. Within those years, I've had to rot in loneliness. It's not fair. You girls have never been attracted to me. I don't know why you girls aren't attracted to me, but I will punish you all for it. It's an injustice, a crime, because . . . I don't know what you don't see in me. I'm the perfect guy and yet you throw yourselves at these obnoxious men instead of me, the supreme gentleman.

By the time the video was posted, Rodger had already stabbed three men to death. He then uploaded the video, dispatched a 107,000-word manifesto called *My Twisted World*, got into his car, and drove to a sorority house at the University of California, Santa Barbara. He pounded on the locked door but couldn't get in, so he shot three female students on the street. Two of them died. Then he drove through the town of Isla Vista shooting at more random victims and targeting them with his car. Before the rampage ended, fourteen people were injured and six others were dead.

This was obviously the act of a diseased mind and horrifying on the face of it. What is more horrifying is that Elliot Rodger became an instant folk hero. On incel message boards he is sometimes called a Supreme Gentleman, a patron saint. Violence against women is called "Going ER." And the cult worship is not merely theoretical.

Alek Minassian, the Toronto man charged with killing ten people by ramming them with his van in April 2018, had taken to Facebook just before the attack to address his inspiration, Elliot Rodger. "Private (Recruit) Minassian Infantry 00010, wishing to speak to Sgt 4chan please. C23249161. The Incel Rebellion has already begun! We will overthrow all the Chads and Stacys! All hail the Supreme Gentleman Elliot Rodger!"

William Atchison, who walked into his former New Mexico high school in December 2017 and shot two students to death, used the pseudonym "Elliot Rodger" online. In November 2018, Scott Beierle, an incel who had invoked Elliot Rodger in an online video, walked into Hot Yoga Tallahassee and opened fire. Six women and one man were shot. Two of the women died. More perversely still, in the aftermath of mass shootings, such as the 2017 Las Vegas massacre that claimed fifty-eight lives, the incel message boards lit up with speculation, hoping that the shooter was one of them.

This grab bag of perversities and pathologies, connected only by mutual resentment for the powers that be, is not just a freak show. It is now a voting bloc. In 2016, the alt-right was Donald Trump's base, united in little but a shared sense of humiliation and cultural impotence—a sense which, as we have seen, has been building for decades as society has remedied inequities to the chagrin of many in the dwindling majority.

Scholars have long debated whether populism feeds more on economic security or perceived loss of power and social status. Nazi Germany, after all, grew in a climate of post-WWI national humiliation, but also the hyperinflation and unemployment of the Weimar Republic. Modern research tools, though, have yielded some clarity. In a detailed 2016 study of populist movements in thirty-one Western democracies, professors Ronald F. Inglehart of the University of Michigan and Pippa Norris of Harvard's Kennedy School crunched survey data and exit-poll results and rendered a judgment: The greater vulnerability is cultural displacement. "Older birth cohorts and less-educated groups support populist parties and leaders that defend traditional cultural values and emphasize nationalistic and xenophobia appeals, rejecting outsiders, and upholding old-fashioned gender roles. Populists support charismatic leaders, reflecting a deep mistrust of the 'establishment' and mainstream parties who are led nowadays by educated elites with progressive cultural views on moral issues."

So when a candidate proclaims himself to be the only answer—"I and I alone"—to your twin pillars of worry and suspicion, you tend to feel that your voice, yours as an individual, is at last being heard. As Mrs. Willy Loman told her kids about their prideful, disappointed wreck of a father, "Attention must be paid!" And so Trump did. To the litany of resentments built over sixty-some years, and to the immediate sense of economic insecurity, all of which he blamed on the same liberal elites.

In a paper titled "Of Cultural Backlash and Economic Insecurity in the 2016 American Presidential Election," American University professor of government Paul Christopher Manuel observed how well candidate Trump ministered to the slighted. "He promised to institute policies predicated on economic nationalism, to stop the flow of jobs overseas. He also promised to fight terrorism, to make the country safe. At the Republican national convention, he notably promised that, 'I am going to bring back our jobs to Ohio and Pennsylvania and New York and Michigan and all of America and I am not going to let companies move to other countries, firing their employees along the way without consequence. Not going to happen anymore!' "

He would take on the foreigners. He would take on the corporations. He would take on (you know what "globalists" means, right?) the Jews. And the Muslims and the hordes of Mexican rapists and the "Deep State" and the lying media. He would take them on to Make America Great Again, while God parted the clouds.

It's all, in one sense, so surreal—even contrived, along the lines of the unbearably sanctimonious 1992 Tim Robbins cinema screed

Bob Roberts or even more so the 1957 Elia Kazan film *A Face in the Crowd*, which starred Andy Griffith (!) as a folksy singer whose populist themes and political cunning propel him to frightening heights.

The criticism of these films is that they are alarmist and exaggerated, even ham-fisted, in their plots and portrayals. But they apparently sensed something. In the convergence of insecurity, human nature, demagogy, celebrity obsession, and ever-repeating history, they recognized inevitability. To wit: the distillation of zeitgeist grievances into a persona that seems to understand and validate a whole spectrum of individual, put-upon, resentful "me"s. No subtlety required. No intellectual honesty, much less rigor, required. For the disparate self-diagnosed victims of cultural oppression, Trumpism was O-negative: the universal donor. It had to happen. It did happen. And for a reason utterly unrelated to politics, it happened at the worst possible time.

PART II

MASS EXODUS

4

The Doomsday Machine

Who ever thought we'd miss the corporate fat cats—the exclusive club of media conglomerates who divvied up the TV, magazine, and newspaper audience into a few gigantic chunks? I'm speaking of Gannett, Hearst, Times Mirror, Cox, CBS, Disney, Time Inc., Condé Nast, Knight Ridder, Gulf + Western, Washington Post Company, Advance Publications, McGraw-Hill, NewsCorp, and New York Times Company, which for decades fed on 30 to 40 percent profit margins lavished by the finite but enormous treasury of advertising dollars.

The corporate leviathans weren't as colorful or as politically heavy-handed as the press-baron likes of Joseph Pulitzer or William Randolph Hearst, or as dynastic as the Chandlers, Ochses, Bancrofts, Binghams, and Paleys, who were civic institutions unto themselves. But in a rapid, disco-era flurry of consolidation, when Walter Annenberg sold his Philadelphia newspapers to Knight

Ridder, and when the Chandlers sold Times Mirror Company to the Tribune Company, and when the Paleys sold CBS to Westinghouse (which was flipped soon thereafter to Viacom), and when Gannett snapped up some one hundred and fifty local papers in an unprecedented acquisitions spree, the character of the media business was transformed. What had been managed locally was now managed nationally. What had been privately held family businesses became public corporations subject to the ebb and flow of the stock market. What had been particular to its environment and its ownership became more homogeneous.

The journalist-turned-academic Ben Bagdikian frantically waved a red flag. In his 1983 book *The Media Monopoly*, he called the media sector a cartel. This not so much for economic behavior; there was no need for newspapers or magazines or TV stations to unfairly protect their monopoly or duopoly markets from competitors because the barriers to entry took care of that problem for them. Broadcast towers and printing presses and delivery-truck fleets and gigantic rolls of paper are very expensive. It required a lot of capital to compete with, say, the *Los Angeles Times* for only a presumably thin slice of a basically finite advertising-revenue pie.

What the concentrated media sector did have an undue influence over, Bagdikian believed, was political dialogue.

> At issue is the possession of power to surround almost every man, woman, and child in the country with controlled images and words, to socialize each new generation of Americans, to alter the political agenda of the country. And with that power comes the ability to exert influence that in many ways is greater than that of schools, religion, parents, and even government itself. . . . Government's passivity has emboldened the new giants to boast

openly of monopoly and their ability to project news, commercial messages, and graphic images into the consciousness and subconscious of almost every American.

In other words, hegemony: a handful of networks, newspapers, and magazines commanding vast audiences and dictating both the national agenda and the boundaries of political decency. The charitable explanation is that they took seriously their role as gatekeepers. Under that rationale, it was an act of civic responsibility to deprive oxygen to extreme views and to limit debate to the fat part of the bell curve—what pollster George Gallup called "the jaws of consent." Or perhaps, as Bagdikian preached, they were invested too deeply in the status quo and fearful of upsetting the most profitable apple cart ever. In either interpretation, these media juggernauts were the de facto arbiters of acceptable speech, acceptable politics, and acceptable thinking. The hallowed "free market of ideas" turned out to be highly regulated—by plutocrats and corporations answerable only to their shareholders. To Bagdikian and a community of political scientists, media economists, and historians, this was a crisis in the making, a gathering catastrophe for democracy and the free exchange of ideas.

Gee, how quaint.

The Bagdikian passage I quoted was actually lifted from the fifth edition of *The Media Monopoly*, published in 1997. That was concurrent with the earliest rapid growth of the internet, which surely seemed to render all of his fears and objections moot. The handful of media owners were suddenly joined by millions of message boards, websites, and blogs whose barrier to entry—the investment required to compete for the audience's attention—was $0. Which is quite affordable.

By the time YouTube and the Facebook News Feed came along in 2006, the internet was already hosting the ultimate democracy of ideas—even undemocratic ideas. Sure, the big media companies were still gatekeepers, but it was a lot like the desert tollgate in *Blazing Saddles*, an easily avoidable obstacle in the vast expanse of the Wild West. The supply of viewpoints, no matter how centrist or extreme, was inexhaustible.

Only one problem with that: Due to the pesky laws of economics, an inexhaustible supply leads inevitably to absolute can't-keep-my-eyes-open fatigue in demand. Remember, the media business is the advertising business. Strictly speaking, the product is not the publication or program; it is the audience, and the customers are advertisers who among them pay $600 billion a year worldwide to attach their messages to news or entertainment "content." So let's do some arithmetic. Let's say there were fifty thousand ad-supported businesses around the world, each feeding on that pot of $600 billion. Not bad, $1.2 million apiece! Now, suppose there were ten million such media entities. Hmm. $6,000 apiece.

Only it's worse than that because, once again, supply and demand: As the opportunities to reach audiences have so vastly expanded, the more bargaining power is afforded the brand customers, and thus less any given media property can command for any given unit of its space or time. CPMs, the unit price to reach one thousand sets of eyeballs, have been driven down, down, down. As they say in the business, analog-ad dollars have been replaced by digital-ad dimes. This is your media economy in 2020. Obviously, large media with large audiences continue to generate significant revenue, and they augment ad dollars with subscriptions, events, and other relatively small income streams, but they are nonetheless all fighting for an ever-narrower slice of a shrinking pie.

But, wait. It's even worse than that. Because, in round numbers, Facebook and Google alone account for $150 billion of the entire ad market, leaving $450 billion for everyone else. Of that $450 billion, $150 billion goes to non-Facebook/Google digital publishers, and half of *that* is eroded by ad-tech middlemen, bots, and criminals. So, in effect, the entire media ecosystem outside of Facebook and Google shares not $600 billion but $375 billion. Many, many more media businesses—from Comcast to Lyrics.com—are vying for the same scraps, like seagulls on the boardwalk fighting over a French fry. And just for one more finger in the eye, the most lucrative segment of the newspaper business, classified ads, has been eradicated by Craigslist, LinkedIn, and a half dozen job-posting and resume-posting sites. (More on this in chapter 7.)

Not that this is a mere newspaper-business problem. In December 2017 came a little-noticed financial story. Verizon, the gigantic telecom, wrote down its $4.6 billion investment in Oath, which was the combination of AOL and Yahoo, which once upon a time were dotcom unicorns raking in cash like craps players on a Vegas hot streak. "Wrote down" means acknowledging that Oath was worth only half of what Verizon paid for it when it decided (foolishly) to enter the media sector. But it could have been worse, as Bloomberg News reporter Scott Moritz observed in his coverage of the writedown. "The episode offered a silver lining for investors. Rather than attempt a megadeal like AT&T Inc.'s $85 billion acquisition of Time Warner Inc., Verizon only spent about $9.5 billion in the past three years buying fading web giants. Though the bet hasn't paid off, it at least stumbled on a smaller scale."

On one day in January 2019, layoffs were announced at Verizon Media's *HuffPost* and AOL (eight hundred jobs), Gannett (four hundred jobs), and BuzzFeed (15 percent of their workforce).

On the same day, the Bend, Oregon, *Bulletin* filed for Chapter 11 bankruptcy.

Because the media business sucks. And that is why your local paper doesn't send a reporter on road games with your local MLB team. That is why all the copyeditors have been laid off for a decade. That is why it publishes in print only three days a week. This is why your broadsheet has been shrunken to the size of *My Weekly Reader*. That is why it doesn't have anyone covering the suburban school boards, or the water and sewage authority, or the statehouse. If your local paper happens to be *The New York Times*, it doesn't even cover local crime. Yes, *HuffPost* and BuzzFeed are sucking wind, too, but for local news consumers the stakes are so much higher.

A 2018 University of North Carolina School of Media and Journalism study documents the toll of the digital revolution:

- Some 1,800 newspapers—more than one in five—have been shut down over the past fifteen years. Of the nation's 3,143 counties, half have only one paper, and it is most likely a small weekly. The vast majority—around 5,500—have a circulation of less than 15,000. About 200 counties have no paper at all.
- Of the 7,100 surviving newspapers, many are "shells, or 'ghosts,' of their former selves."
- Two-thirds of the nation's daily papers are owned by chains, dramatically retrenching to cut costs amid shrinking revenue.
- Over the same fifteen years, overall circulation plummeted from 122 million to 73 million.
- Thousands of communities have become, or are at risk of

becoming, news deserts, with no access to local, regional, or state news reporting.

News deserts, those barren expanses of info-desolation, where citizens don't know how their tax money is being spent, or who is being sued or arrested or married or born, or what caused the fire or fatal car wreck or which elected official is illegally lining his pockets. Because nobody is watching and nobody is telling.

In 2010, the *Los Angeles Times* ran a series documenting a five-year conspiracy by city employees and elected officials of Bell, California, to swindle millions of dollars from taxpayers. The city council of the largely low-income L.A. suburb (population 35,811) had passed ordinances, levied taxes, and padded budgets, allowing them to pay themselves off-the-charts salaries and benefits. The city manager, for instance, was compensated to the tune of $1.5 million a year. The crooked officials managed this because nobody—public or press—ever went to Bell City Council meetings, including the *L.A. Times.* The local *Wave* weekly, with one reporter to cover fourteen municipalities, did its journalistic watchdogging by calling officials after meetings to get a synopsis. Strangely, those officials never mentioned pillaging the treasury. A *Times* reporter stumbled on the scandal while reporting on the financial distress of a neighboring suburb, during which a pseudonymous blogger tipped them off about Bell's insane payroll. Then some fine journalism broke out, but not before five years of corruption hid in plain view.

The Flint, Michigan, water crisis offers a similar cautionary tale. In April 2014, the cash-strapped city of Flint—in the process of switching from the Detroit Water and Sewerage Department to the less-pricey Karegnondi Water Authority—saved $5 million to $7 million in the interim by pumping water from the Flint River.

Complaints about the water's taste and appearance arose immediately, but the criticism was pooh-poohed by city and state officials and got little attention from the struggling *Flint Journal* or *Detroit Free Press*. One reporter did stay on top of the story, however. He was Curt Guyette, whose employer was the American Civil Liberties Union. Concerned that fundamental problems in Michigan were receiving too little scrutiny from the local media, the ACLU had secured a Ford Foundation grant to bring in a journalistic private eye. Guyette accompanied an out-of-state scientist who canvassed Flint, documenting abnormally high levels of lead in tap water, and uncovered an EPA memo that revealed state lead-content data was misleadingly reported as low. Only then, in September 2014, after five months of poisoning, did the shit hit the fan. Blood tests on children revealed elevated lead exposure, which causes diminished intellectual capacity. Within a month, the state spent $12 million to switch Flint back over to water from Lake Huron.

It's not that mainstream news organizations were asleep at the switch. It's that there are too many switches to monitor. In 2004, according to the Bureau of Labor Statistics, there were 71,640 full-time editorial employees at American newspapers. Today there are fewer than 33,000.

So one catastrophic problem is that fragmentation and a ruinous content glut have yielded less journalism. A related problem is they have yielded worse journalism. Trivia. Infotainment. Clickbait. Whether the latest news on the Kylie Jenner–Kim Kardashian feud, or speculation on the next iPhone or even the continuous stream of palace-intrigue gossip from the Trump White House, we are inundated with more and more of less and less. *Remember these child stars? What they look like now will make your jaw drop!* Because, unlike the news documenting the activities of government and industry, gossip is cheap to produce and extremely seductive to the audience. Even in the realm of cable (so-called) news, there is vanishingly little actual journalism but rather endless prime-time jawboning about what others have reported. In the actual marketplace of ideas, legislative redistricting and offshore shell companies can't begin to compete with live partisan shouting matches, much less Kim Kardashian's ass. Meantime, climate change is pushed to the back (planet) burner and regulatory apparatuses designed to protect the public are being systematically razed with little attention from the press. Apart from the Mueller investigation, the U.S. government has become Bell, California.

Mind you, this is not a new complaint.

We know things are bad—worse than bad. They're crazy. It's like everything everywhere is going crazy, so we don't go out anymore. We sit in the house, and slowly the world we are living in is getting smaller, and all we say is, "Please, at least leave us alone in our living rooms. Let me have my toaster and my TV and my steel-belted radials and I won't say anything. Just leave us alone." Well, I'm not going to leave you alone. I want you to get mad!

That was the primal scream of the fictional, disgraced anchorman Howard Beale in the 1976 movie *Network*, raging against complacency, cheap titillation, and the conglomeration of everything, including the media. Then he told viewers to "get up right now and go to the window, open it, and stick your head out and yell, 'I'm as mad as hell, and I'm not going to take this anymore!'" But the public wasn't, and didn't. It voted for fluff with its eyeballs and then with its clicks.

I spoke of Ben Bagdikian's version of media concentration as quaint. You know what else seems just adorably naïve? The notion of technology as the solution to Bagdikian's—or Howard Beale's—alarm. In 1989, Ronald Reagan predicted "The Goliath of totalitarianism will be brought down by the David of the microchip. . . . The communications revolution will be the greatest force for the advancement of human freedom the world has ever seen." And then came vice president Al Gore, famously touting his "information superhighway":

> This form of government became possible, according to many, only after the printing press distributed a sufficient quantity of civic knowledge to empower the average citizen to participate in the decisions that were necessary to guide the destiny of a great nation. If that was the case, then we can only imagine what advances for democracy lie in store.

Gore and others did plenty of imagining about the blessings of the internet—just as Robert Moses and Dwight Eisenhower and General Motors imagined the benefits of actual concrete superhighways. The failure of imagination, however, concerned the other side of the equation, namely the unintended consequences. In the case of physical roads: the carving up of cities and populations into sectors of haves and have-nots, the isolation of suburban life, and the poisoning of the earth's atmosphere. In the case of the internet: fragmentation, rampant incivility, fraud, privacy violation, identity theft, hate speech, propaganda, and—as predicted by absolutely nobody—a form of media concentration such as even Ben Bagdikian couldn't have imagined. "All of a sudden," says Jonathan Taplin, director emeritus of the Annenberg Innovation Lab at the University of Southern California and author of *Move Fast and Break Things*, "what you have is a world in which there are two or three gatekeepers who have far more concentration of power then Walt Disney in its wildest imagination ever had."

By "or three" he means maybe one of them is Apple. But by "two" he means the duopoly, Google and Facebook.

Let us contemplate the Facebook News Feed. It's where you can find photos of your "friends'" kids, cat gifs, funny memes passed along by your pals, fake news stories designed by provocateurs to rile you up and confirm your worldview, actual news stories from legitimate news organizations, fluffy content from those same outlets, and, of course, ads—ads most likely targeted at you based on your geolocation, demographic, and psychographic data you have volunteered wittingly or unwittingly, your own behavior online measured and stored click by click, keystroke by keystroke. It's a pretty good business. In 2018, Facebook's ad sales generated $40 billion worldwide. Google did $100 billion. After adjusting for global ad dollars lost to middlemen and fraud, the duopoly claims 31 percent of the world ad market. In the United States, according to the trade group Digital Content Next, *every dollar of growth in the advertising market* goes to Google and Facebook.

"Facebook and Google, for the most part, don't create any content," says DCN's CEO Jason Kint, "and so, 100 percent of the growth in the industry is going to two companies that don't create any content."

But they do have an audience—of billions—and, as such, they are by far the biggest distributors of news and news-like content in the world. This has some benefits, beginning with the enormous reach it gives publishers and the shared ad income that comes with it; when you click on a *Washington Post* story on Facebook, the *Post* gets a small cut. That business model, however, also has some positively dystopian disadvantages, mainly the ceding of distribution to third parties who have no journalistic or civic mission whatsoever. These tech companies' interest is in keeping you personally glued to their platforms, a motive that doesn't lend itself to feeding users with the latest on thawing permafrost or Aleppo or anything whatsoever taking place in your statehouse. What it favors is dresses that look gold and white to some people and black and blue to others or Kanye's nervous breakdown or fake news.

Not that vast boiler rooms of Facebook curators are making decisions about what to include in or exclude from your News Feed. That service is performed by the EdgeRank algorithm, the computer code that serves you not what it perceives as a balanced media diet, but what it knows you've been interested in before. Google News and YouTube do the same. If you've been a good boy and eaten your whole grain and vegetables in the past, you will be served more whole grain and vegetables. If you've pigged out on comfort food and dessert, that's what you'll get.

And if you've clicked on bogus conspiracy content manufactured by partisan scoundrels or Russian agents, yes, you'll get stuff like Pizzagate, 9/11 "truthers," Obama-is-a-Kenyan-born-Muslim "birthers," "exposés" about George Soros's (nonexistent) Nazi collaboration, Sandy Hook deniers, and this gem: "Welcome to the Hillary and Bill Clinton body count documentary. In this video, we're going to discuss the 114 people the Clintons have killed to keep quiet."

Fake news, of course, is not a twenty-first-century invention. Indeed, before the mid-twentieth century professionalization of newspapering and decoupling from party affiliation, it was a staple of the press since the founding of the republic. But what is unique to our times is the filter bubble of our social media accounts, which, like lazy parents, keep feeding us more and more of what we like, whether good for us or not—with the twin repercussions of fueling hate speech and lies and depriving us of reliable information. You don't have to be an ivory tower academic to see how this can contaminate the democracy. But just in case, I have one of those eggheads right here:

"Things have to push emotional buttons with a whole lot of strength to really carry through Facebook's ecosystem," says Siva Vaidhyanathan, professor of media studies at the University of Virginia. "And the effect that it's having on us is clear. It is hurting our ability to operate as citizens in a republic. It's hurting our ability to make sense of the world. It's harming our ability to think through complex problems."

You might ask then why legitimate news organizations would be part of an ecosystem that gouges them in the revenue sharing and favors competing content, no matter how scurrilous. The answer is, it's for the same reason Sunglass Hut pays onerous rent at the mall: That's where the shoppers are. Half of publishers' traffic comes not to their home pages but through aggregators like Google News and social media. And so, in cities around the country, in search of eyeballs and the ad revenue that comes with them, papers are scrambling to locate readers wherever they happen to be and to serve some content that most intrigues them.

"What's trending," says Neil Chase, executive editor of the Bay Area News Group, whose San Jose flagship is the *Mercury News*, "in terms of what's being talked about on other websites, not so we can do the same things but what are we missing, what are people talking about?"

Chase says the days of editorial mandarins dictating story selection are long gone. Not only must the *Mercury News* take its content wherever the readers are, it must take it where the readers' interests are.

> There are certain stories that we will cover whether or not we think they're interesting to people, but there are also stories you look at and think, 'I don't know if we really needed to cover that story, let's have a thoughtful conversation about whether that's the kind of news we should be covering.' The second layer is, what's happening on our site? Which things did well over the past twenty-four hours or over the past weekend? What got people's attention, what didn't because we didn't write the headline the right way or we missed something? And if we're not thinking about every headline and writing it well, then we're not getting that story in front of as many people as want to see it.

Which, in a click economy, is what keeps the lights on: stories that get seen generate ad revenue, however diminished. (Publishers get half their traffic from social media, but only 14 percent of their revenue.) But maybe readers will be drawn back to the newspaper's homepage, generating more page views. Maybe they'll sign up for a newsletter or buy a reprint. Every little bit helps. And every little bit, Chase emphasizes, subsidizes the expensive and generally less lucrative nuts-and-bolts reporting at the core of the newspaper's mission.

Or not. Because the paper's hedge-fund owners are mercilessly slashing payroll, and the staff for fulfilling the noble mission is shrinking like a dick in a cold bath. Oh, and the click economy it surrenders to is a perfect medium for Russian intelligence to toy with our elections. Neil Chase certainly sounds like a thoughtful man acting thoughtfully to make the best out of a situation over which he has little or no control. But I've heard words like that before, from editors in Venezuela and Russia and Central America and South Africa and the Middle East, all trying to navigate onerous obstacles, erected by authoritarian masters, to sneak some journalism to their readers. The Facebook-ization of everything, wrote John Herrman in *The New York Times Magazine* just before the 2016 election, is a "slow-motion coup."

In the next chapter, we'll discuss filter bubbles—the segregation of information according to ideology, often directly resulting from the Facebook algorithm. It is another confounding paradox: the fragmentation and isolation of media consumers resulting from the immensity of a single beastly duopoly. This is not just a bad social outcome, and a bad economic outcome, according to internet pioneer Tim Berners-Lee, it is a bad *network* outcome antithetical to the history and healthy future of online life. "Close to the principle of universality is that of decentralization," he wrote in 2010, "which means that no permission is needed from a central authority to post anything on the Web, there is no central controlling node, and no single point of failure."

But if Berners-Lee is right, and Bagdikian was right, and Vaidhyanathan and Taplin are right, and if the temple has been overrun by the moneylenders and partly for that reason a new dark period of political history has been ushered in, wherein too much power has, indeed, been usurped by a small number of people, the irony is thick. Back in the 1950s, the computer age itself was ushered in largely according to the ethos of the philosopher-mathematician Norbert Wiener, father of cybernetics. According to Stanford University communications professor Fred Turner, Wiener sought safe haven for democratic discourse in the wake of fifteen years of fascism *via exactly the architecture we now call the filter bubble.* It was a utopian vision, says Turner, "in which freedom was imagined as being able to build your own feedback loops, as being able to enter into the world, seek the information that you needed, learn from it and then change your action accordingly. In many ways, Google is the dream of Norbert Wiener . . . realized. The trouble is, once realized, it doesn't necessarily bring us democracy. It brings us a new and different mode of authoritarian enclosure."

Yes, an unintended consequence of utopian engineering, like genetic modifications going haywire in the wild or *Dr. Strangelove*'s Doomsday Machine. Recall Peter Sellers as Strangelove, in his wheelchair in the Pentagon war room, describing the technology that took human judgment out of the loop in nuclear confrontations: "Because of the automated and irrevocable decision-making process which rules out human meddling, the Doomsday Machine is terrifying and simple to understand—and completely credible and convincing."

Convincing, like a dubious business proposition that sounds like a good business proposition; convincing, like an invented presidential endorsement from the pope in Rome; convincing, like cyber sirens luring us to their irresistible but fatal pleasures. Odysseus lashed himself to his mast to fight that temptation. Howard Beale became unhinged. In *Dr. Strangelove*, it was the end of the world.

5

Bubble, Bubble, Toil and Trouble

We don't see things as they are; we see them as we are.

—ANAÏS NIN

Ever do some online shopping for, say, a pair of shoes or a wine stopper or an inflatable sex partner and soon find yourself stalked by ads for the very items you browsed for? That's called "retargeting." Marketers know if they keep putting their merchandise in front of you, you are more likely eventually to surrender and buy those teal stilettos or Love Doll or whatever. The odds for making a sale are so much better, in fact, that they assume the risk of creeping you out big-time for weeks or months until some percentage of their targets finally cave. The data tell them that. If you of your own volition opt in to look at something on the internet, the internet knows to keep feeding you more of the same.

It works that way for shopping, and it works that way for content. The internet is like Santa. It knows when you are sleeping, it knows when you're awake, it knows when you're downloading porn, and it knows if you love Drake. Moreover, and more to the point, it knows where its best interests lie.

Facebook and YouTube don't sell merchandise. They sell attention—yours—to their advertisers. The more time you spend on their sites, the more and more pricey advertising they can sell, so naturally they benefit from serving you with content most likely to keep you sticking around. In fact, the term they apply to such content is literally "sticky."

Now maybe you say, "No, no. I scroll down my Facebook News Feed and there's all kinds of stuff there posted by my friends, and stuff I follow. I can choose whatever I want." Yeah . . . no. Only a very small portion—under 5 percent—of what your friend and follow networks put out there ever winds up on your feed. What does show up there is determined by EdgeRank, the Facebook algorithm, dictated by data it has on you and your previous content choices. If Aunt Bernice keeps sending you photos of her wall-eyed dog, Violet, and you keep scrolling past it, soon Aunt Bernice will vanish from your feed—replaced by stuff similar to what you've clicked on before, such as perhaps scrapbooking ideas or college basketball or Hitler. If you commented on a post, the likelihood of getting more of the same is greater. If you shared, even greater. Most social media platforms have their own versions of EdgeRank to achieve the same benefit.

YouTube celebrity Anthony Carboni, host of "The Star Wars Show," a direct beneficiary of ranked feeds, has reflected on Twitter about what it looks like in the online wild:

Me: *watches a single YouTube tutorial so I can fix my door hinge*

YouTube: WHAT'S UP, HINGE-LOVER? HERE ARE THE TOP 1000 VIDEOS FROM THE HINGER COMMUNITY THIS WEEK. CHECK OUT THIS TRENDING HINGE CONTENT FROM ENGAGING HINGEFLUENCERS

Hahahaha! "The hinger community." That's his own host platform he's making fun of (and—just sayin' is all—the way his own show gets fed to likely audiences). He's imagining the most absurd extreme of what's called a "feedback loop," or, as internet entrepreneur and activist Eli Pariser famously dubbed it a decade ago: "filter bubble." It applies, however, not only to cute shoes and *Star Wars* geeks. It applies as well to things that very much matter. Such as, for example, a cruel stroke of medical misfortune.

Imagine if you were to have a son who seems healthy and normal at birth, but who soon develops symptoms of autism. It's a heartbreak, of course, not only because the child faces a lifetime of struggle, but for you, as you now are destined to a lifetime of care and shattered expectations of the normal cycle of life. Will your boy ever leave the nest? Will he marry? Will he give you grandchildren? Will he have normal life expectancy? Will he ever even be self-sufficient? Will he be happy?

And naturally also the nagging question of what happened. Why him? Where to place the blame?

Science has no answer to that question, even as the incidence of autism keeps skyrocketing, from 1 in 150 children in the year 2000 to 1 in 59 today. Something must be causing it . . . but what?

In 1998 came a paper in the esteemed British medical journal the *Lancet* that seemed to offer an answer that question. Written by a physician named Andrew Wakefield and twelve coauthors, the article relied on twelve case studies to suggest a link between autism spectrum disorders and the measles, mumps, and rubella vaccine. It was not a major account of a rigorous double-blind experiment, nor even a major article in that edition of the *Lancet*, but it was noticed by the press and the story blew up. A link between a universal vaccine and autism? A danger! A culprit! A sensation! In the British press over seven and a half months, there were 521 stories on the study.

During that same period, Wakefield came under scrutiny for careless research methods, not to mention the cardinal sin of mistaking correlation for causation. (Yes, the autistic kids had been vaccinated for MMR, but they also ate bananas, listened to lullabies, and wore socks. Yet socks were not accused of damaging children's brains. And then, of course, there were the 99.5 percent of kids who got the vaccine and did not have autism.) Eventually it became clear that Wakefield—whose research had been funded by law firms retained by autism families to sue vaccine makers—had misrepresented and fabricated data. The *Lancet* eventually retracted the study, and a host of scientific and medical institutions, including the National Academy of Sciences and Britain's National Health Service, refuted any link between autism and MMR. Wakefield lost his medical license. But it was too late. The damage had been done. As Cardiff University communications scholars Tammy Speers and Justin Lewis found in their 2002 study of the Wakefield press coverage, the vast majority of reporting was of the he-said/she-said variety, casting the issue as a mere difference in scientific opinion. From their report:

What is missing from much of even the more balanced coverage is any sense of the weight of scientific evidence, which is firmly stacked on the side of those who support MMR. The impression created by most of the reports we looked at is merely that there is conflicting evidence on this issue.

As it often does with widely disseminated misinformation, and when the press defaults to false balance, the public internalized the idea that there was legitimate scientific debate on the subject. By the time the *Lancet* retracted the article, eleven years had passed and in the interim hundreds and thousands of heartbroken parents had come to believe in a smoking MMR gun. A global community of so-called anti-vaxxers had long since coalesced online. Their fears and suspicions, like MMR itself, went viral. Jenny McCarthy, the ex-*Playboy* model and TV personality, became the face of a gathering movement. The attention paid to her was based on her son Evan's neurological disability and her other credential of being a smoking-hot blonde. And she made for provocative TV. "Without a doubt in my mind," she told CNN, "I believe that vaccinations triggered Evan's autism."

On ABC's *The View* Dr. McCarthy dispensed medical advice: "People are also dying from vaccinations. Evan, my son, died in front of me for two minutes. You ask any mother in the autism community if we'll take the flu, the measles, over autism any day of the week. I think they need to wake up and stop hurting our kids."

And how did she know enough about immunology to advise parents to roll the dice with measles, mumps, and rubella? Well, she explained to Oprah, she was a student in good standing at "the University of Google."

A Google shout-out and a Facebook wet dream. Anti-vaxxers

weren't just clicking; they were sharing. And here's what happened as a consequence: Smart moms like Jenny McCarthy stopped vaccinating their children. In the United Kingdom, MMR vaccine compliance in 1996 was 92 percent. In 2003 it was 61 percent. And measles, mumps, and rubella—which had been largely eradicated—came roaring back. In the year 2000, there were 86 cases of measles in the United States. In late April 2019, more than 700 cases had been diagnosed in twenty-two states. As this paragraph is being written, the state of Washington, amid a measles outbreak, is in a state of emergency. In Europe, in 2018, there were 41,000 measles cases and 33 deaths.

Two decades after Wakefield's fraudulent article, belief in this lethal dose of junk science has yet to be dislodged. Like Sasquatch and supply-side economics, the myth endures. And why? Because it persists in the minds and feedback loops of the people whose very personas are tied up in MMR paranoia. It is their identity, their Members Only jacket. So, in early 2019, when the avowedly arch-conservative TV station chain Sinclair Broadcast Group obliged its stations to run a "documentary" on vaccines, claiming to reveal previously hushed-up information on "one of the biggest medical controversies of our time," it knew it was pandering to the paranoia of the members. Among mainstream media, where the bias is toward controversy and the principal sin of laziness, this direct assault on truth is an anomaly. In social media, it is a business model.

In 2014, researchers Douglas Badenoch and Giordano Pérez Gaxiola conducted an experiment. They opened several Facebook accounts and searched for "vaccine harms." When presented with suggestions for relevant groups and pages, they "liked" the first choices offered—one account steering toward anti-vax hokum, another toward science.

> Within three clicks of the search results we identified three anti-vaccine pages with over 125,000 "likes." Very quickly, our timeline was populated with anti-vaccine information. After "liking" an article, four more anti-vaccination suggestions appeared, all with over 10,000 "likes." Our comparisons revealed a different Facebook experience according to opinion (pro- or anti-vaccine), location and language.

It was, they concluded, a confirmation-bias engine. And, as Anthony Carboni joked, the same goes for YouTube, where the right-rail recommendations within three clicks inevitably lead users to conspiracy content—a phenomenon known in Silicon Valley as "Three degrees of Alex Jones." In sum, we are not learning or speaking to one another; we are isolated on tiny islands in a vast Filter Bubble Archipelago, endlessly validating our own worldviews—a zillion preachers charging up a zillion choirs.

And it is worse still. Because once entrapped in the bubble, we are resistant to any information or view that conflicts with our own personal certainty—even if it comes from a media source we are inclined to trust. A 2018 Gallup/Knight Foundation experiment followed the online preferences of 11,695 participants on a custom-built aggregation platform offering articles from the ideological spectrum of media—from Media Matters and Vox on one end and Breitbart News and 100 Percent Fed Up on the other. Some of the subjects were showed the content and asked to rate it for trustworthiness on a five-point scale. Others were shown both the content and the trust ratings of "the community" and "people like you." Still others were shown the content and a history of their own trustworthiness ratings. The experiment yielded a strange but eye-opening conclusion:

> This analysis finds clear evidence that, concerning media trust perceptions, people appear to change their attitudes when presented with metrics conveying others' opinions. The difference between a person's past attitudes and the general attitudes communicated via the community or "people like you" averages causes cognitive dissonance that ultimately affects overall media trust perceptions adversely.

In other words, if people like you trust an article more than you do, you respond by trusting the article even *less*. Faced with the differing perspectives of others, the subjects retreated more deeply into their own ideological reflexes. We reside in bubbles, validating and revalidating our mutual worldviews. But when we face resistance to our beliefs, we withdraw still further into a bubble containing only ourselves. In such a perverse prison of self-validation, we make terrible decisions. And children die.

And, for the same set of reasons, democracy is on life support. Eli Pariser predicted as much in *The Filter Bubble: What the Internet Is Hiding from You*:

> Ultimately, democracy works only if we citizens are capable of thinking beyond our narrow self-interest. But to do so, we need a shared view of the world we cohabit. We need to come into contact with other people's lives and needs and desires. The filter bubble pushes us in the opposite direction—it creates the

impression that our narrow self-interest is all that exists. And while this is great for getting people to shop online, it's not great for getting people to make better decisions together.

Please note that the Gallup-documented changes in trust did not flow from the verifiable truth or falsity of the content. In the bubble, facts are no match for belief. There is no Democrat Party child-sex ring being operated out of a Washington, D.C., pizzeria, and never was. There is no fleet of UN black helicopters poised to invade the capitals of the world and steal their sovereignty, and never was. There was no U.S. military operation under the Obama administration to overthrow Texas and jail patriots in a vacant Walmart (I'm pretty sure we already *have* Texas, don't we?). There was no George W. Bush administration plot to blow up the Twin Towers on 9/11 as a false-flag operation. There was no fake moon landing. Baby Barack Obama was born in a Honolulu, Hawaii, hospital, just as the birth certificate and contemporaneous newspaper announcements said.

And at Sandy Hook Elementary School in 2012, having already shot his own mother to death, Adam Lanza murdered twenty children and six adults. It was not a hoax. No matter what that asshole Alex Jones or his addled followers believe, the victims' grieving parents were not "crisis actors" in a plot to undermine the Second Amendment. It was a fucking massacre conducted with a fucking assault rifle such as the fucking NRA has fought for decades to be readily available.

In each of these matters, there is an easily accessible body of evidence—plus plain common sense—that renders the conspiratorial ravings manifestly preposterous. The web of supposedly damning details (often themselves false or invented) may seem provocative to those predisposed to believe in vast malign forces, but of course those meticulously constructed webs include none of the context: the countless obvious and documentable facts Alex Jones and his like somehow leave out. Such as, in most of these episodes, dozens or hundreds or thousands of eyewitnesses. But filter bubbles are not places given to, shall we say, intellectual rigor. The process of accepting even the most dubious scenarios when they conform to our established beliefs is what social scientists call "motivated reasoning." And once motivated to ignore evidence, the true believer tends to stay motivated to embrace still more hogwash—what *Republic of Lies* author Anna Merlan calls a "domino effect of the mind." Ever wonder how any sucker, no matter how naive, could fall for the Nigerian 419 Fraud con, where the honorable recipient of a flowery email is offered a vast fortune from the estate of some African tribal chieftain/government official if only they'll show good faith by ponying up banking info and $50,000? The answer is: because they wish, against all evidence, to believe it's true. Indeed, that is the core of all confidence games: predisposition. Honest people can't be grifted. It's not just that victims are merely dupes. They are greedy dupes, who value desire over reason.

Conspiracy theory consumers are so ideologically greedy they suspend disbelief.

This holds true even when the individual's portfolio of paranoia is internally contradictory. And once the narratives are inserted in Facebook filter bubbles or subreddits, to be traded among like-minded communities, suspension of disbelief goes begging. As Turkish techno-psychologist Zeynep Tufekci reminds us, "Belonging is stronger than facts." Which is why the bubbles are shoot-first/don't-ask-questions-later zones. And what zones they are.

Consider "Morgellons syndrome," a disorder in which textile

fibers are said to sprout out from human skin. It is by medical consensus a psychiatric issue, along the lines of delusional parasitosis, but those hip to the hidden architects of world domination attribute it to government-deployed nanobots and "chemtrails"—which, of course, aren't benign airplane condensed-water contrails but rather clandestine sprays of toxic agents deployed by sinister arms of the government, duh.

"Someone needs to investigate this government/medical cover-up! Were these parasites also clandestinely and aerially sprayed upon the unknowing population of Northern California?" wonders a blogger named Ricardo Beas. Or could it be what Ole Dammegard speculates about on his *Light on Conspiracies* site?

"The best theory I've heard so far is that these are being created by some type of hellish nano technology that uses the body to grow the fibers and get its energy from the body also. Are they trying to turn humans partly into machines by growing fibers inside of us that can eventually be used to control us or just kill us? I don't know the plan here but clearly it's from satan and it's hellish in nature."

The commenter Vendi LaRose totally got the Morgellons plot: "They are spraying us with them in the Chemtrails. IT's deliberate for their transhuman agenda."

Widespread Morgellons hysteria finally triggered a CDC investigation that in 2012 yielded unsurprising results: no infection, no pathogen, no parasites, no nanobots, no transhuman agenda. "Most materials collected from participants' skin were composed of cellulose, likely of cotton origin." Plus: a fair amount of nail polish sticking the cotton fibers to the "eruption" sites. But in filter bubbles, where certainty is abundant, due diligence is in short supply. As Gallup said to conclude its 2018 media-trust study, "It seems that the more people know, the more skeptical they become."

In the spring of 2018, *Politico* ran a story about a particular item of fake news that had reached hundreds of thousands of people. The phony headline was this: "BREAKING: First Full Supreme Court Ruling in Over a Year Has Obama FURIOUS."

It claimed that the U.S. Supreme Court had banned "Sharia Law and Islam from being taught in classrooms." Now this was obviously untrue for many reasons, not the least of which is that the Establishment Clause of the First Amendment already would prohibit Islam or any religion from being practiced or advocated in school, but would equally permit freedom of speech to teach *about* it. Second, no case even remotely like it had been percolating in the courts. Third, the story referred to a nonexistent "17th district" federal court. And the language in the article—"a direct and final blow to the Islamic Indoctrination of the young in this nation"—sounds like it was written by a Klansman and/or fifth grader. So naturally hundreds of thousands of people took it as fact and shared it hither and yon—because, they thought, it was finally some good conservative news that was obviously being suppressed by the liberal media.

The article, which had been bouncing around the internet for months at that point, was the work of a supposed "satire" site called America's Last Line of Defense, which publishes similar provocative, semiliterate content either as some sort of *Colbert Report*–esque postmodern commentary (as it claims), or to generate clicks from gullible partisans for the ad revenue they provide, or maybe both. Anyway, this one was a viral bonanza.

Politico tracked down a number of people who posted it on social media accounts, all of whom believed they were spreading good news, not fake news. One was a guy named Kurt Withrow, who had posted it on Facebook with a favorable comment—and got pushback, or even a question, from exactly zero of his nearly eight hundred friends. Not a single peep of disapproval or disbelief.

Why? Because, in their social media bubbles, they weren't exposed to any content that would impeach it. And because they were predisposed to believe it. And because the story validated not only their views, but their very selves. Jonah Berger, Wharton School marketing professor and author of *Contagious*, told *Politico* that sharing a piece of highly partisan content is yet another form of social signaling. Another set of tailfeathers, another Steelers bumper sticker, another bar call of Ketel on the rocks, three olives. As Berger described the thinking, "What does it say about me to share this thing? Just like the car we drive and the clothes we wear says something about us."

A sense of belonging, a sense of self, and more than that, a sense of self-importance. Like the Safety Patrol. Or the glee club. Or the brownshirts. Or the liberals.

Yes, the liberals, who dwell in feedback loops, as well. We, too, construct our worlds largely around likeminded people, and we, too, immerse ourselves in certain categories of information. Now I will say categorically that *The New York Times*, *The Washington Post*, *The Atlantic*, *The New Republic*, *Slate*, and NPR are not the same as Fox News, Breitbart News, the *Daily Caller*, Rush Limbaugh, and the rest of the right-wing attack media, which are not just partisan but political weapons with no interest in facts, context, perspective, or intellectual honesty. Even the explicitly progressive press—Salon, MSNBC, *Mother Jones*, *The Nation*—however strident or condescending or doctrinaire, are seldom accused, much less caught in the act, of fact distortion, let alone faking news.

It is undeniable, however, that our Facebook News Feeds and Twitter feeds and YouTube accounts are approximately as filtered and homogenous as those of conservatives. Also our home libraries and dinner tables and picnics. If anyone in our circles casually announced, "Yeah, I like Trump," I promise you cervical vertebrae would snap as heads swiveled in synchrony, amazement, and horror. We may some of us take pride in reading the *Wall Street Journal* editorial page or *National Review* online or *Commentary*, just to get a sense of the intellectual underpinnings of ideology we find incorrect or even repugnant, but we don't go out to dinner with these people—or, if we do, we make a show of our tolerance, like Spencer Tracy in *Guess Who's Coming to Dinner*. This is called elitism. And it is often blamed for the 2016 presidential election results—not because all those fine news organizations we favor failed to traipse all over red America documenting nascent Trumpism. The press did yeoman work reporting far-flung dissatisfaction in what now is known as Trump Country and duly reported the polling that reflected such anger, as well. Maybe Trump's electoral victory wasn't predicted by the polls, but it wasn't inconsistent with the polls, either, or the reporting on the ground. The data made him a long shot, and the long shot came in.

However, however, however . . . there is what liberal America knew and what we believed, or wished to believe. The commentary, the body language, the premature anointing of the first woman president did not project the intellectual honesty of which we are so proud, and which we so lord over the political right. What was projected was arrogance, self-satisfaction, tone deafness, and exactly the kind of elitist superiority that so infuriates red America in the first place. We could not hide our smug confidence. It simply oozed from our filter bubbles, like something out of *Ghostbusters*, and it was not lost on Wisconsinites, Ohioans, Pennsylvanians, and Floridians. Trump may or may not be Mussolini, but he is definitely Dr. Peter

Venkman, a charismatic fraud who got the public to believe him. Not because he made sense, but because they so despised the fancy government big shots (like *Ghostbusters*' "dickless" EPA rep Walter Peck) who saw through him. Their contempt for us, in other words, fed off our perceived contempt for them. Yes, our fractured politics are the direct toll of filter bubbles. But you can't safely confine your analysis to conservative America. It's like crossing the street. First look left. Even the Russians did that.

In the last two weeks of 2018 came a pair of reports prepared for the Senate Intelligence Committee by a collection of technology consultants, social media analysts, and university researchers. The gist of the combined sets of findings was this: Russian intelligence agents, via a St. Petersburg company called the "Internet Research Agency," actively employed social media platforms to seed discord before, during, and after the 2016 president election, with a goal of damaging Hillary Clinton's prospects and advancing Donald Trump's.

This from the report by Renee DiResta, Dr. Kris Shaffer, Becky Ruppel, David Sullivan, Robert Matney, and Ryan Fox of New Knowledge; Dr. Jonathan Albright of Tow Center for Digital Journalism at Columbia University; and Ben Johnson of Canfield Research, LLC:

> Throughout its multi-year effort, the Internet Research Agency exploited divisions in our society by leveraging vulnerabilities in our information ecosystem. They exploited social unrest and human cognitive biases. The divisive propaganda Russia used to influence American thought and steer conversations for over three years wasn't always objectively false. The content designed to reinforce in-group dynamics would likely have offended outsiders

who saw it, but the vast majority wasn't hate speech. Much of it wasn't even particularly objectionable. But it was absolutely intended to reinforce tribalism, to polarize and divide, and to normalize points of view strategically advantageous to the Russian government on everything from social issues to political candidates. It was designed to exploit societal fractures, blur the lines between reality and fiction, erode our trust in media entities and the information environment, in government, in each other, and in democracy itself.

That, of course, was hardly big news. The degree of Russian interference in the 2016 election has been the subject of Senate and House investigations and special counsel Robert Mueller's probe since Trump took office. What was new was confirmation, and granular detail, of the specific tactics employed by the Russians to sow political and social discord. The IRA opened accounts under fake American identities on a dozen social media platforms and created websites for nonexistent activist organizations supposedly dedicated to social justice for one or another aggrieved constituency. The harvest, according to the New Knowledge report: 10.4 million tweets across 3,841 Twitter accounts; 1,100 YouTube videos across seventeen account channels; 116,000 Instagram posts across 133 accounts; 61,500 unique Facebook posts across eighty-one pages. The three top platforms generated in all 337 million user "engagements."

Much has been made of the systematic pandering to seething conservatives, which certainly took place, but a bigger focus was on African Americans and the #BlackLivesMatter movement, through phony sites such as blackmattersus.com, blacktivist.info, and blacktolive.org.

The IRA created an expansive cross-platform media mirage targeting the Black community, which shared and cross-promoted authentic Black media to create an immersive influence ecosystem. The IRA exploited the trust of their Page audiences to develop human assets, at least some of whom were not aware of the role they played. . . . The degree of integration into authentic Black community media was not replicated in the otherwise Right-leaning or otherwise Left-leaning content.

"Human assets," the report said—which is intelligence jargon for "spies," in this case mainly unwitting—cultivated by intelligence officers to infiltrate the enemy. With a history of affinity for the Clintons, black voters were a strategically crucial part of the electorate to turn against both Clinton and the political process in general. Of the eighty-one spoof Facebook pages created by the IRA to masquerade as aggrieved American interest groups, thirty were aimed at the black community, whereas twenty-five were aimed at the entire political right.

The strategy was to get their attention, get their trust, and then to get their anger focused in the proper—that is, beneficial for Trump—direction. To the authors of the second Russian-interference report to the Senate Intelligence Committee—Philip N. Howard, Dimitra Liotsiou, and Bharath Ganesh of the University of Oxford and John Kelly and Camille François of Graphika—it was all reminiscent of the Arab world in 2011. "It is certainly difficult to tell the story of the Arab Spring," they wrote, "without acknowledging that social media platforms allowed democracy advocates to coordinate themselves in surprising new ways: to send their demands for political change cascading across North Africa and the Middle East."

The 2016 Russian assault was essentially a funhouse-mirror

image of the Arab Spring. That revolt against authoritarian Arab regimes was famously fomented on Twitter, but not because citizens spontaneously signed up to the platform to tweet "Mubarak Must Go." No, as organizer Mona Saif told me from Tahrir Square in an interview for *On the Media*, people were already on Twitter posting messages about the trivia of everyday life: meals, travels, media, romance, gossip. They had already forged trusted relationships. So when the stakes got high—political freedom itself—the bonds preexisted for evolution into a movement.

"When these people are following you," Saif told me in 2011, "and suddenly you are talking about a torture case, some of them might not usually be exposed to such cases. But because they are following me and there is an ongoing conversation between us, they would suddenly be engaged in this, as well."

In the case of the Arab Spring, that dynamic was a serendipitous side effect of shared lunch JPEGs. In the Russian intelligence operation, it was engineered. Credibility was first earned with posts about genuinely shared grievances—such as a video of cops roughing up a black pedestrian.

PLEASE HELP THIS VIDEO GO VIRAL. THESE COPS CAN BEAT UP INNOCENT MAN, GET AWAY WITH MURDER EVEN WHEN IT'S CAUGHT ON CAMERA JUST BECAUSE THEY WEAR A 'MAGICAL' BADGE AND GUN.

This generated 539,012 shares. And then, having amassed followers, the IRA fed highly inflammatory fake news and ad hominem attacks. On October 29, 2016, a week before the presidential election: "NO LIVES MATTER TO HILLARY CLINTON. ONLY

VOTES MATTER TO HILLARY CLINTON." On November 3: "NOT VOTING is a way to exercise our rights."

It was, to paraphrase Ronald Reagan's taunt to Mikhail Gorbachev, a case of "trust, then vilify." And black participation in the election was the lowest in two decades. Whether that was a consequence of Russian voter repression, or GOP voter suppression, or yet other factors is unknowable. What is knowable is that our adversaries inflated filter bubbles, populated them, and watched in delight at the freak-out. They did the same with veterans, Christians, and, naturally, racists and xenophobes. From the sock-puppet Twitter account @secured_borders:

> If we want to REALLY end these "sanctuary cities", we should start hauling handcuffed city officials who are accessories to the crime! Perp walk mayor blowhard into a FEDERAL slammer on prime time news. THAT will get this "sanctuary" crap over with in quick time!

> Arrest them—the mayors, police chiefs, governors; prosecute them, don't give them bail, make them sit in jail and then sentence them to prison—see how many of them are willing to be ruined and go to jail—they will change their tunes once they realize that the rule of law is ruling again.

> No city in the U.S. should be a sanctuary for illegal alien scum, period!

All, once again, in the service of a candidate believed by the Russians to serve its own interests. This, once again, from the Oxford-Graphika report to the Senate:

The IRA sowed both secessionist and insurrectionist sentiments, attempting to exacerbate discord against the government at federal, state, and local levels. . . . The IRA had a very clear bias for then-candidate Trump that spanned from early in the campaign and throughout the data set. A substantial portion of political content articulated pro–Donald Trump sentiments, beginning with the early primaries. Aside from an extremely small set of early posts supporting Rand Paul, this preference was consistent throughout the Right-leaning IRA-created communities.

The Oxford University scholars call it "computational propaganda." I call it social espionage. But Russia is not the only interest this tradecraft serviced. The other beneficiary was the Facebook-Google duopoly—the new hegemons—who host the filter bubbles, power the filter bubbles, and lavishly profit from the filter bubbles. And did so all through the election period, and continue to do so now. Both Senate reports document ongoing Russian activity on social media, especially on (Facebook-owned) Instagram, still mainly in service of Trump and Trumpism. Yet, according to the researchers who briefed Congress, those companies were only marginally cooperative in providing the internal data useful for assessing the scope of the social espionage.

The reluctance may be to protect themselves legally, or to protect themselves politically. And maybe also financially. Because the consumer-behavior data held by them literally quantifies human nature, the value of which knowledge is incalculable. They know, probably to thirty decimals, the level of craving for provocative content, much as scientists can quantify a lab rat's preference for cocaine-spiked water over plain. They know the relative velocity and scale of "engagement," and they know precisely how resistant the inhabitants of a filter bubble are to ideas that conflict with their own hardened truth.

Think of that Gallup study. Even when confronted with contrary evidence and opinions from those we trust, we still dig our heels more deeply into our own beliefs, even if we must inhabit our bubble all alone. There is a word for that, too: *paranoia*. And it is an epidemic. Violence has sent nearly a million human beings fleeing for their lives. In Myanmar, thousands of ethnic Rohingya have been murdered and raped—not by soldiers, but by angry Buddhist mobs incited by Facebook posts, clandestinely seeded by the military, alleging immorality, corruption, and terrorism among the Rohingya. These fraudulent posts reached a wide audience because Facebook, in all its generosity, had made basic broadband available for free to poor Burmese citizens so they could enjoy the fruits of instant communications.

Or so they could see ads.

It was a classic test case for the law of unintended consequences. "I'm afraid," the UN's Yanghee Lee declared, "that Facebook has now turned into a beast." That was after the fact, but some Burmese watchdogs had seen the bestiality coming. As the *Myanmar Times* observed when the Free Basics program rolled out in 2016, "Facebook is a force to be reckoned with in Myanmar. It has been used by turns as an election pulpit, fundraising platform, and even an outlet for hate speech."

That warning left Mark Zuckerberg mystified. "Who," he wrote at the time, "could possibly be against this?"

6

Trust Busting

Hate and mistrust are the children of blindness.

—SIR WILLIAM WATSON

Among other progenitors.

—ME

Let us begin with the data.

According to the Public Trust in Government survey from the Pew Research Center for U.S. Politics and Policy undertaken in December 2017, the portion of the public trusting Uncle Sam to do what is right "just about always" or "most of the time" was 18 percent. Among millennials it was 13 percent. Among Republicans—who at the time controlled all three branches of government—it was 22 percent. In October 1964, in the midst of civil rights tensions and the early days of Vietnam, the same question earned government a thumbs-up from *77 percent of all those polled.* If you are scoring at home, 18 percent is a lot less than 77 percent.

An autumn 2017 poll by the University of Maryland and *The Washington Post* found that 36 percent of respondents are "not very proud" or "not proud at all" about how democracy works in America. Some 64 percent said American democracy is dysfunctional. On the question of whether politics have devolved to a "dangerously low point," 71 percent said yes. And 56 percent said there are "fewer things that bind Americans together today than in the past."

Recall, too, the grim laundry list of disaffection from page xii. These findings are piling up. The most recent World Values Survey found that among American millennials, 23 percent say that democracy is a "bad way" or "very bad way" to run the country. In a 2017 survey of five thousand voters by the Democracy Fund, 29 percent of respondents showed at least some support for either a "strong leader" or "army rule."

Army rule.

And it is not just government engendering such suspicion. The Edelman Trust Barometer is an annual tracking study measuring the levels of trust in government, business, NGOs, and media in twenty-eight countries. From 2017 to 2018, its measure of U.S. citizens' trust for those institutions plummeted 37 percent. "The United States is enduring an unprecedented crisis of trust," said Richard Edelman, president and CEO of Edelman. "This is the first time that a massive drop in trust has not been linked to a pressing economic issue or catastrophe like the Fukushima nuclear disaster. In fact, it's the ultimate irony that it's happening at a time of prosperity, with the stock market and employment rates in the U.S. at record highs. The root cause of this fall is the lack of objective facts and rational discourse."

Well, we are certainly experiencing a heyday for irrational discourse and "alternate facts." Donald Trump, Alex Jones, Devin Nunes, Ann Coulter, Dinesh D'Souza, Kellyanne Conway, Sarah Huckabee Sanders, Rush Limbaugh, and the entire Republican congressional caucus inhabit a world in which down is up, up is down, and science is fake news. It is hard for some people to have faith in American institutions when they are being told every day that climate change is a hoax, that Obama is a Kenyan, that the United States government brought down the Twin Towers, that the grieving parents of murdered Sandy Hook kindergartners are "crisis actors," and that Hillary Clinton is splitting time cooking up uranium deals with the Russians and running a child-sex ring out of a pizzeria. Not to mention every word that tumbles from Donald Trump's lying mouth. However, with all due respect to Edelman and the nineteenth-century English poet Sir William, hate and mistrust are not merely the children of blindness. They are also the children of twenty-twenty vision. Distrust in government, media, business, and other institutions of society is not the sole product of internet crazies and Republican liars. It is the product of history, and of information.

Think about the Occupy movement, or the Bernie bros. Or Antifa. Or the democratic socialist following of Alexandria Ocasio-Cortez. These people are not birthers or climate deniers. They are leftists utterly dissatisfied and—to their way of thinking—betrayed by the two-party system, by the boundaries of acceptable debate, by the "jaws of consent." They see the yawning gap between rich and poor, the cynicism of politics, the venality of Wall Street, the perversion of democratic levers for anti-democratic effects, the rape of the planet, the perverse power of super PACs and the NRA, the unchecked power of corporations, and the equivocation and false balance in the media, and they see not just the failure, but the corruption of democracy. And many of them see that is irrevocable. Not because they live in a world of alternative facts, but because they live in a world of damning ones.

Democratization was one great promise of the internet that turned out to be elusive. Another, access to information, very much came to pass.

Yes, the internet and social media gave us fake news. It also gave us the Smoking Gun. TripAdvisor. Yelp. Snopes. These are places where (for the most part) information lives without the intervention or spin or suppression by the reported upon. Yes, the web is a haven for dog whistlers, but also for whistle-blowers. Suddenly we can see documentary evidence that hitherto was locked down by the powers that be. Body-cam video of police brutality. Panama Papers revealing hidden and laundered assets. WikiLeaks, before being co-opted (or worse) by corrupt actors, was where we saw the details of an American helicopter attack on innocents in Iraq, secrets of Scientology, and diplomatic cables documenting the corrupt conduct of Gulf-state allies. The Arab Spring that coalesced over such revelations did so on Twitter.

Online was not where we first heard of torture at Abu Ghraib, but it is where the whole world saw the pictures. And the very same open access that allows cranks, opportunists, and fools to spread lies permits others to spread truths. And voice dissent. And simply complain—not least about the major media and our failures. That is not a short list.

In that Edelman Trust Barometer, the media did not fare well, either. In the 2019 Gallup/Knight Foundation poll, 69 percent of

U.S. adults said their trust in the news media has decreased in the past decade. This is not all hysteria. There are things we must answer for.

Access journalism. Horse race coverage. Herd mentality. Staged cable punditry. False balance. Routine anonymous sourcing. Endless speculation. Cozy relationships with sources. Clickbait. Gossip. Bending over backward to seem less shrill or partisan. Carelessness amid breaking news. And every now and then one of us, like *The New York Times'* Judy Miller, gets played into helping start a war. And every now and then someone like Jack Kelley or Stephen Glass or Janet Cooke or Jayson Blair or Brian Williams gets caught just making shit up.

And all the ugly details are right there. In perpetuity. Not just in media, of course, but the entire breadth of society.

Scoundrels in business and politics, who once operated with impunity safely out of public scrutiny, are no longer protected by impregnable fortresses. Now they are (we are all of us) in glass houses, and our every deed—good and bad—is visible to the outside world. As Don Tapscott and David Ticoll advised businesses in their book *The Naked Corporation,* "You're going to be naked, so you'd better be buff."

Just, for instance, over fifty years, to revisit one of my former journalistic stomping grounds—advertising—United Airlines spent about $37 fucktillion propounding an image of Friendly Skies. But online video of passengers being dragged down the aisle and dogs being suffocated in overhead bins has rendered their image-making a bit dubious. Laughable, actually. "Rhapsody in Blue" is pretty, but it doesn't erase customer abuse on YouTube. (Not that songs can't tell a story. In 2009, Canadian musician Dave Carroll's catchy music video "United Breaks Guitars" started racking up what would become more than 19 million YouTube views. A witty recounting of his band's travel nightmare, it was a rhapsody in "blew it.") For institutions or individuals, the days of dictating image are over, because actual information is right there. And we are not only enlightened; we are mad.

That's because unprecedented access to information yields unprecedented familiarity, and familiarity breeds contempt. Transparency worked too well. We see how the lady isn't really being sawed in half. We see how avuncular Charlie Rose is a creepy old lecher. We see how Father Joe and Doctor Larry are pedophile rapists. We see in fine detail that Wells Fargo and Volkswagen and Cambridge Analytica are conspirators and scammers and crooks at their core. We find out that A-Rod and Maria Sharapova and Lance Armstrong are cheaters. We learn Johnson's baby powder, that fixture of the nursery and medicine chest and dressing table, that cherished icon of childhood, is laced with asbestos—and that Johnson & Johnson has suppressed the truth for decades.

The scales have fallen from our eyes. It doesn't feel good. It is unsettling.

Sorry, William Watson, deceased not-very-gifted poet. The public has indeed seen what it has seen. It has watched the government lie over Vietnam and Iraq and the media credulously pass on those lies. It has been through Watergate and Iran-Contra and the savings-and-loan scandal and the subprime crisis. It has watched public health officials botch the supposed killer flu of 1976 and the Ebola outbreak of 2014. It has watched priests molest and cardinals cover up. It has watched Big Pharma rush bad drugs and devices to market, sometimes on the basis of fudged or cherry-picked scientific data. It has watched beloved and powerful men unmasked as sexual predators. It has watched Bernie Madoff and Enron. It has watched video of unarmed black men and boys gunned down in the street. It has watched both political parties spew rhetoric about the middle class while presiding over an economy, and tax code and federal budget, that systematically favors the rich.

It just hurts. Scandal used to be rare enough to be juicy and entertaining. Now it is ubiquitous and demoralizing. Which is why trust is not merely a state of mind, but a commodity in the marketplace.

But here's the thing: A marketplace is never influenced solely by intrinsic value. There is also investor mood, the stuff of bull markets and bear markets alike. Despair over some institutions has come to affect all institutions. And as surveys by Pew, Gallup, and Edelman demonstrate to a fare-thee-well, just as trust becomes the coin of the realm, we are in a Great Trust Depression. In such an environment, as the surveys so grimly document, democracy itself comes under mass suspicion. And just at the moment the media are most needed as authoritative, honest brokers of facts, context, and perspective, they are at historical lows of public faith and esteem. Yes, we have lost faith in the very institution needed to keep democracy alive. Instead, we turn to friends and family and information sources that share not only our suspicion, but all the idiotic crap that seems to confirm our mutual distrust with the Powers That Be. If this means dismissing documented facts and objective reality, so be it. It feels so courageous and independent and righteous. Even heroic. Not so being on the wrong side of their unshakable suspicion. That's a danger—and irony—reminiscent of the murdered medical missionaries in Afghanistan and Pakistan, trained healers deemed suspicious by virtue of offering life-saving vaccines.

And at the heart of the irony is the internet, which shed sunlight into the darkest corners of the society. And then users looked into its direction and were blinded by the sun.

Or, returning to the idea of fragmented politics and fragmented media, perhaps a related analogy of energy's destructive power: nuclear fission. The constant bombardment of society's nucleus by tiny outside forces yields fission of the most destructive sort. This could lead to a catastrophic explosion and must be interrupted. But how? How? There are six steps, and they are nonnegotiable.

PART III

THE
MANIFESTO

7

Feed the Watchdogs

We as citizens who are sitting around waiting for the next
person on the white horse with the sword to save us ... what
are we doing to be that person on the horse ourselves?

—DAHLIA LITHWICK, on *On the Media*

I f I were God, or the sultan, or just the chief justice, this prescription for change would look very different from what I propose here. *Citizens United* would be overturned. Voting rights
protections would be restored. Partisan gerrymandering would be
legislated and litigated into oblivion. The Electoral College might
be dissolved. But to paraphrase former defense secretary Donald
Rumsfeld, you don't wage a de-devolution with the power you wish
for; you wage it with the power you have. As a matter of both political reality and human mortality, the Supreme Court is out of

reach for a generation. To protect democracy, we must otherwise intervene. This manifesto, therefore, is a platform for change built of six wholly unrelated planks—economic, regulatory, militant, educational, inspirational, harmonious—to counter the forces of ruinous fragmentation. We shall begin with revenue generation.

To start, recall this: For most of three centuries, the mass media economy was a sublime three-way symbiosis. Audiences received free or heavily subsidized content, advertisers got in front of mass audiences, and media—with few competitors to worry about because of huge barriers to entry—enjoyed huge profits. Alas, that ship has sailed. It has sailed directly into an iceberg called the internet. And it is foundering.

In 2006, according to the Pew Research Center, newspaper ad revenue peaked at about $49 billion. In 2017 it was $16.5 billion. Between 2008 and 2017, newsroom employment in print and broadcast fell by 23 percent. And the precipitous decline continues. According to Pew, 36 percent of the largest U.S. newspapers conducted layoffs between January 2017 and April 2018, and so did 23 percent of the highest-traffic digital-native news outlets.

So there's your problem. The collapse of the media economy, and consequent dependence on third-party social platforms, has neutered media's ability to watchdog the society and inform the broad public. How then to restore its vitality? It is a question that has confounded the biggest thinkers in the industry. We are twenty years into the Google era and no ethical, sustainable solution is even on the horizon because there is no immunity from the law of supply and demand. From so-called native advertising (ads dressed up to mimic editorial content) to selling cruises to readers to government subsidies, none of the alternate revenue streams alone or together can replace the bounty of the old model.

Paid subscriptions are slowly increasing, but consumers are accustomed to—and generally insistent on—getting content for free. More on this subject presently. Yes, the cruises, the book clubs, the reprints, the merchandise, and the (I swear to God) dating services do provide welcome incremental income, but they are a rounding error in the overall newsroom budget. Conferences and other live events have become a bigger and bigger slice of the revenue pie, but they also face a growing conference glut and typically low rate of return on investment. Data has cash value, but publishers are loath— partly over privacy concerns, partly over cost of building up sales infrastructure, and partly for fear of losing competitive advantage— to sell it to third parties. Cooperation with Facebook and Google has come with high costs and piddling revenue. The nonprofit model works for public broadcasting, and has a (very) few pockets of success around the country, but depends on a finite amount of noblesse oblige and stiff competition from the opera, the museum, the Vietnam vets, and every disease under the sun. Do we really want to inhabit a world in which the local paper is in competition with the Leukemia & Lymphoma Society?

That so-called native advertising, in which publishers work with advertisers to create worthy "content" that looks exactly like the adjacent journalistic material, has yielded a significant revenue stream and some percentage of well-crafted content—*at the enormous risk of killing the goose that lays the golden egg*. Apart from the high marginal cost and low profit potential of this stuff, "native" is fundamentally deceptive. It is essentially advertising disguised as editorial, trading not on its own merit but on the hard-won credibility of the publisher. It doesn't merely trade on it, it *barters that trust away* story by story. Never mind golden geese, the practice reminds me of nothing so much as Nauru, the Micronesian island whose bustling post-WWII economy was built entirely on the phosphate resource (i.e., crusted seagull shit) that covered the island. For a half century Nauru shipped away its guano to the fertilizer industry, until there was no more guano to sell. It is now destitute.

Then there's the business model I call "the patient billionaire"— mainly internet tycoons who invest in a dubious business proposition out of a sense of civic responsibility. There are a few who have raced to the rescue for *The Washington Post, Boston Globe, Los Angeles Times, Time* magazine, and *The Atlantic*, but that is a vanishingly small population and, once again, the Billionaire Boys Club faces many an outstretched hand. (Furthermore, the white knights can't necessarily be seen as pure. The late Rev. Sun Myung Moon, Sheldon Adelson, Philip Anschutz, and the late Richard Mellon Scaife all bought papers explicitly to flog ideology, which is true to our history of Revolutionary-era pamphleteers but antithetical to the principles of modern journalism. See chapter 9.)

In the interest of offering life support to local news operations, the state of New Jersey and other jurisdictions have toyed with the idea of government subsidies, which sounds swell . . . if you want your journalism financed by the government it is reporting on. "He who pays the piper . . ." and all that. Even back in the old days, peeved local officials would withhold statutorily mandated (and highly profitable) legal ads from local papers that had gotten under their skin.

In short, it's a hellscape out there. All the king's horses and all the king's men have worked this problem for two decades, and so far (to cite literally the oldest punch line I know) the yolk's on them. As a student of media ecology, I see only two potential solutions. One concerns the willingness of the audience—contrary to current behavior—to pay for more of the content it consumes, through means I'll get to shortly. The other is out of the audience's hands, but not out of the marketplace's hands. It concerns technology.

What if publishers can bring in more income not by expanding the advertising market, necessarily, but by eliminating billions of dollars lost to waste and fraud? You will recall a bit of arithmetic from chapter 4, calculating that about one-eighth of the global advertising spend—$75 billion—is diverted from publishers to ad-tech middlemen and crooks.

For example: Consider the scheme tracked down by Craig Silverman of Buzzfeed News in October 2018 (and subsequently shut down by Google) involving a company called Fly Apps. Through a complex web of offshore shell companies, it amassed at least 125 legitimate phone apps that were downloaded 115 million times by consumers and operated as designed. This allowed the owners to harvest highly granular behavioral data on its users—whereupon bots disguised as human users and mimicking their behavior began "clicking" on in-app ads. The shell companies then charged advertisers for the fake traffic at a cost to the system at least in the tens of millions of dollars.

The amount lost to fraud globally is actually uncertain. In a 2015 study by the Interactive Advertising Bureau underwritten by ad-tech companies, the estimate of fraud was valued at $4.6 billion. In 2016, the Association of National Advertisers and the bot-detection company White Ops estimated it at $6.5 billion. In 2018, Juniper Research, the British digital consulting firm, estimated $19 billion. However, that is on top of the "ad tech tax," which is the amount siphoned off legally by various players in the digital-ad supply chain. In programmatic ad buying—where computers bid in real time to place an individual ad before an individual user—eMarketer estimates the vig to be 60 percent of the $80 billion spent worldwide, or

$48 billion. That adds up to $67 billion, which doesn't account for shrinkage in the remaining $70 billion spent on non-programmatic digital buys worldwide.

"There's a messy, porous supply chain; it's a source of confusion and vulnerability; and a lot of companies don't have a clue how their sausages get made—or what goes into them," says Randall Rothenberg, CEO of the Interactive Advertising Bureau, who says the problem is his "biggest hobbyhorse." He believes the scale is far lower than some alarming estimates, but he also worries about the risks taken by his members, risks he attributes to their calculation of cost versus benefit:

> One of the biggest reasons you don't find a lot of companies publicly pulling back and narrowing their [ad-tech and trading-platform] partnerships is that more of these seemingly unnecessary middlemen have become essential to their businesses. They provide forms of analysis they can't get elsewhere, they help them take charge of crucial advertising and marketing distribution processes in-house without having to own the underlying technology, they allow them to become creators and distributors of marketing and entertainment product themselves.

This is my analogy, not his, but a similar justification is used for paying protection money to the mob. Just sayin', is all.

Anyway, let's say the total shrinkage is $75 billion. That's a lot of money. On Christmas Day 2018, it was enough to buy 37.5 billion Santa Claus Pez dispensers (with Pez). Or you could have bought every share of Gannett, Tegna, the Tribune Media Company, and

Charter Communications, plus only 1.69 billion Pez Santas. The idea is that some or most of that $75 billion could be recouped and recirculated in the actual media economy.

To be clear, the *news* media economy is but a fraction of the media sector, dwarfed by entertainment, search, online, and the rest. But the opportunity still applies: If advertisers have more to spend and are looking for safe spaces to spend it, news publishers will benefit.

There are various methods for doing so. One is for advertisers and publishers both to severely limit the number of platforms where they trade. Most ad deals are consummated on ad *exchanges*, which are something like cattle auctions, where the owners of the various livestock parade their inventory before many prospective bidders. In that scenario, the cattlemen are the publishers, the bidders are the advertisers, and the ads are the cows. The problem is, in ad exchanges, the bidders are blindfolded. Nobody knows who is buying from whom, and nobody gets to inspect the cows. It is an efficient system for buying and selling at optimum price, but it adds a layer of ad-tech-tax cost and is uncomfortably opaque.

The opacity problem is even greater on ad networks, which are digital advertising's bargain bin. You know the cows that just got sold? Well, eventually they wind up in supermarkets, where their carcasses are butchered for sale. They get packaged in foam trays with plastic wrap and sit in the meat case until someone buys them. When the packages are still sitting there as the expiry date approaches, the supermarkets will mark them down for quick sale. That is an ad network. It is also efficient, but once again the networks take their percentage of every transaction. Furthermore, another layer of middlemen are arbitrageurs who buy cheap inventory, then often repackage it and resell it for large markups to incautious brands. And in every transaction there is a very high risk of purchasing spoiled meat.

Furthermore, in each stop along the programmatic trail, not only cost but JavaScript is appended to every ad, creating delays on page loading called "latency." It's why you sit there waiting excruciating squandered seconds for that picture of Meghan Markle to come up—you know, the one where she's rocking that hot outfit that made Kate Middleton just so enraged.

There is currently a move afoot to create *publisher* exchanges, disintermediating the other platforms and allowing advertisers to deal directly with publishers—or, at least, the publishers' computers. It could help. Although please note that one of the major players being disintermediated is DoubleClick, owned by Google, which is not likely to just roll over and die. Furthermore, on the subject of monopolies, removing layers from the supply chain also reduces the number of competitors, which historically has not been a benefit to marketplaces. (See chapter 4 and chapter 8.)

Another possibility is the confusing—but also actually kind of simple—technology known as the blockchain. You may recognize that as the guts of Bitcoin and other cryptocurrency, but in its essence a blockchain is merely a ledger, just like one you'd find at a bookkeeper's office or the tax office at the courthouse—except that it isn't written on tightly spaced paper pages with consecutively numbered entries in indelible ink and stored under lock and key. Instead it is an uncopiable, unerasable list of transactions recorded through digital information packets called blocks and distributed to thousands or many thousands of computers on its network. Both parties have access to the information through cryptographic keys. And because it is a distributed network, there is no central repository for hackers to attack to alter or contaminate the ledger.

Many companies are attempting to bring this technology to the advertising supply chain as a means to create transparency in a chaotic marketplace. Just for example, in the matter of abusive arbitrage, it would keep track of the costs paid for an impression on an ad network, and follow it through to the final buyer to see if, say, Ford Motor Company were getting gouged. Or, as often happens, paying for a page that loads as a pop-under on a website and is never seen by human eyes. The blockchain can much complicate attempts at "domain spoofing," in which crooked publishers digitally masquerade crappy pages to seem like premium sites and fetch top dollar for nearly worthless ad impressions. And, perhaps most of all, it could render largely unnecessary some of the many layers of expensive ad tech deployed precisely to sniff out fraudulent impressions.

The problem with existing blockchain technology is that it is relatively slow. It can process thousands of transactions per second, compared to the programmatic marketplace processing millions. Speed and capacity would have to increase by orders of magnitude before a ledger-governed marketplace could liberate much of the hijacked $75 billion for spending with legit publishers. Still, there remains another blockchain-driven possibility: the creation of new mechanisms for exchanging value.

The first is the most obvious: micropayments. Remember that the most common application of distributed-ledger technology is cryptocurrency, such as Bitcoin, which can enable tiny, frictionless remittances to publishers in exchange for content now impossible under expensive, cumbersome payment systems like credit cards. Card transaction fees are large and would most of the time cost more than the actual price of a content consumed. Crypto transactions, by contrast, are essentially free. In a more developed crypto world, media consumers could, with a click or swipe, pay pennies for an individual piece of content, permitting à la carte consumption of content free of advertising altogether. Or it could enable "tips," voluntary payments from news consumer to publisher over and above an existing advertising or subscription model. *Hey,* Akron Beacon Journal. *Loved your Saturday story about the Aurora-Wadsworth girls basketball game. Here's a little something extra for you* . . .

This capacity must await far more universal adoption of Bitcoin, which is not so far a particularly fluid or ubiquitous marketplace, and one notoriously subject to wild fluctuations of value. But it is slowly gaining awareness, and traction.

At the same time, another application of blockchain commerce is evolving in the so-called attention economy. Blockchain has the ability to commodify actual audience attention, converting it into credits in the form of crypto tokens. By means of the underlying ledger, advertisers can be assured that such attention has actually been earned—a potentially transformational alternative to an extraordinarily inefficient status quo, in which advertisers pay for impressions without certainty that anybody has been, uh, impressed.

The best approximation till now, for TV broadcasters, has been the Nielsen ratings, which measure what content is tuned in to at any given hour in American households. But it is at best a rough proxy for actual attention verification. Who in the household is actually watching? Are they sticking around for the ads, or running to the kitchen? Are they muting the sound? Are they watching at the time of broadcast, or catching up via DVR—and if so, are they fast-forwarding through the ads? On such squishy data tens of billions of ad dollars are spent. But what if you could actually measure and certify audience attention?

Once such version is the BAT—Basic Attention Token—through which an advertiser pays BATs to both the publisher and the consumer based on how long an actual ad has actually been viewed. BATs are convertible to legal tender, or for the purchase of premium content wherever BATs are traded. At the moment, this marketplace is limited to Brave, the free, open-source browser that made a name for itself by automatically blocking ads, but which is changing its business model to accommodate the attention economy. Another pioneer is the social media tech company SocialFlow, which analyzes social feeds to help publishers find the optimal time and place for posting their stories. Its Universal Attention Token similarly rewards publishers and users for actual ad consumption. Purveyors of both tokens say they will create a better user experience—lower ad load, fewer annoying paywalls, and token access behind those walls where they do exist.

When and to what degree will these technological advances actually advance? Who knows? But it won't be tomorrow, and in the meanwhile, today is a bloody mess. For the foreseeable future—five years, let's say—the media economy is (1) ill-equipped to fulfill the basic First Amendment functions the founders envisioned, and (2) getting weaker all the time. The advertising that you always hated did more for you than you most likely realize. It paid for *The Beverly Hillbillies* and coverage of the Kennedy assassination, the Pentagon Papers, Hurricane Katrina, and the Arab Spring. It pays for the Super Bowl, *60 Minutes*, and *Wizard of Id*. It pays for your YouTube stars and your Instagram. As noted media theorist Mary Poppins put it, "It takes a spoonful of sugar to help the medicine go down." *Young Sheldon* is the sugar. Advertising is the medicine.

The whole history of mass media, in fact, has been one of advertiser subsidy. A copy of a newspaper cost more than a penny to produce in 1833 when the "penny press" was born, and it costs more than $1 to produce today. A copy of *Vogue*, with its glossy paper and high-end fashion photography, has always been sold at a newsstand price (now $6.99), representing a fraction of its actual cost. Network television costs millions of dollars per episode; you get it for free. Thank you, Procter & Gamble.

The reason, of course, is that the value of the mass audience to mass marketers was for centuries so great that they could pay high advertising rates, which underwrote nearly the whole kit and caboodle. Subscriptions and per-copy sales added revenue, obviously, but were actually more important to show advertisers that the audience cared enough about the content to pay for it (free publications fetch, and always have fetched, lower ad rates than paid ones). It was a highly beneficial ecosystem for all parties involved, until the internet hobbled it in five devastating ways:

1. Those mass audiences became much less massive, as the number of media outlets soared exponentially and fragmented the audiences among them.

2. The vast number of media choices created a supply glut, which dramatically eroded the price publishers/broadcasters could command per thousand members of their audience. When you hear of plummeting "CPMs" (cost per thousand), the supply/demand imbalance is why. Obviously, a smaller audience times a lower ad rate equals revenue calamity.

3. For newspapers, the most profitable ads were classifieds, which were all but obliterated by Craigslist, Autotrader, Monster.com, ZipRecruiter, et al.

4. Whether by DVR skipping or spam filters or online ad blockers—not to mention the phenomenon known as "banner blindness," in which the reader doesn't even register the

ads on the periphery of the screen—ad avoidance became not only possible but routine. While it somehow became a twentieth-century commonplace that "the commercials are better than the shows," the fact is that advertising has always been regarded mainly as a nuisance. The moment audiences had the opportunity to avoid them, they did so in droves. To the consumer, all advertising is spam.

5. The widely believed notion that "information wants to be free." That ethic, attributed to *Whole Earth Catalog* founder Stewart Brand in 1984, was meant as an argument for unfettered access—that is, freely available, not "free of charge." Brand and others believed that copyright and other intellectual-property protections were too broad, yielding mini-monopolies that stifled progress, but they were not communists or lunatics. If you wanted a copy of the *Whole Earth Catalog*, you still had to pony up cash on the barrelhead.

Nonetheless, the catchy expression came to be understood, and internalized, as the internet as a free commons where nobody really owns anything. This, as you might imagine, in addition to being irrational, was a bit troublesome for industries that invest hundreds of millions of dollars to create the content. The likes of Napster, and the piracy it encouraged, destroyed the record business—destruction that neither iTunes nor Pandora nor Spotify has fully undone.

Legacy publishers took note of what had taken place in music and made a historically disastrous strategic decision. Believing that users would be resistant to buying subscriptions for their content, they chose almost across the board to give it away online for free, with the assumption (or blind hope) that the gigantic reach of the internet would generate larger audiences and therefore much more ad revenue, rendering subscription revenue unnecessary. For why that was a colossal blunder, see items 1 and 2 above. But by the time the folly of that strategy had become apparent in the new millennium, the public had become fully accustomed to "free of charge" and demonstrated little enthusiasm for contributing. When paywalls went up, by and large, the public simply went elsewhere for their content. Now *HuffPost* is no *Washington Post*, but whatever, it's gratis.

The exception to the rule is *The New York Times*, which has signed on nearly three million digital-only subscribers and one million for the digital-print combo. Together, they bring in just above $1 billion, compared with $558 million in total ad revenue. In 2018, that yielded common shareholders a profit of $125 million—or a margin of 7.2 percent, versus the good-old-days margins in the 30 to 40 percent range. And to get there, the company has had to slash payroll and other costs annually for a decade—which means fewer reporters, fewer editors, many fewer foreign and domestic bureaus, and dramatically limited metro coverage in its own backyard. This, ladies and gentlemen, is the industry's success story.

Hence, the urgency. We cannot wait for the blockchain, or artificial intelligence, or six hundred freshly minted billionaires to come to the rescue. We need you. To pay your way. Now. This isn't called a manifesto for nothing. It's both a declaration of core principles and a set of marching orders. Yours is as follows:

Subscribe to your local newspaper. Donate to your public radio and TV stations. If you read *The New York Times* or *The Washington Post* or *The Guardian* or the *Chicago Tribune* online, subscribe to them. In point of fact, journalistic information is not free. It is dear—in every way. If you complain about fake news but don't pay for real news, you are part of the problem.

Face the facts: You are a freeloader. Stop that. Not only are you sponging on other people's labor and investment, you are an accessory in starving the watchdogs. Don't starve the watchdogs. Nourish them.

Or, to once again switch metaphors, take note of *The Washington Post*'s slogan: "Democracy dies in darkness." Someone has to pay the bills, or the lights go out. So pay the bill. Now. Literally. Right now.

8

No, Really, Trust Busting

Our current predicament cannot be wholly blamed on a suffocating media sector. It cannot be wholly blamed on filter bubbles, trapping citizens in the prison of their own worldviews. It cannot be wholly blamed on Russian sabotage of our presidential election. Hard not to notice, though, that all three of those disabling conditions can be laid at the feet of Facebook.

One giant octopus of a corporation, responsible for so much of what ails our democracy.

Facebook has been the conduit of hate speech and lies big and small. It has been the stifler of exchange in the marketplace of ideas. Along with duopoly twin Google, it has sucked 25 percent of the revenue out of the global advertising economy, crippling the rest of the media industry. It has allowed mercenary and prying hands—including Cambridge Analytica—to invade our privacy and then hidden its own culpability. It has for its entire history made unilateral changes in its relationships with both users and media "partners." It engineers its every pixel to manipulate human behavior in the direction of actual addiction. It profits handsomely off of the flood of phony, dishonest, demagogic speech that literally drowns out reasoned debate. And it is the location of the Filter Bubble Archipelago, the sprawling chain of identity islands, where the likeminded comfort one another with shared grievance, shared ideology, shared suspicions, and shared certainty. These nearly impenetrable digital redoubts are the intentional, algorithmically cultivated harvest of Facebook's "engagement strategy." Which I'd call an entrapment strategy.

Oh, and on top of everything, even in the midst of crisis, even after investigators had proven its platform was exploited for the nefarious benefit of an authoritarian U.S. adversary, it remained opaque about its operations and its trove of data. In the Oxford/Graphika report on the Internet Research Agency—the principal Russian saboteurs of the 2016 election—the authors seem incredulous at Facebook's minimal cooperation in the investigation. The company actually disabled access to the data interface (API) governing non-ad posts, even though they are where most of the mischief occurred.

"The loss of access to the API for public post data prevents further public understanding of the latest trends in computational propaganda," the authors complained. "Facebook provides an extremely limited API for the analysis of public pages, but no API for Instagram. Facebook provided the U.S. Senate with information on the organic post data of eighty-one Facebook pages, and the data on Facebook ads bought by seventy-six accounts."

It was as if the researchers were channeling the jurist Louis Brandeis, who in 1912 said this about omnivorous monopolies: "I should say over and over again, we need knowledge—comprehensive, accurate, complete knowledge of what is being done in business. And the striking fact today is the absence of such knowledge."

Did you ever see *The Jerk* with Steve Martin? The premise is that a country bumpkin blunders into a simple way to keep eyeglasses from sliding down the bridge of the nose and becomes stupidly wealthy with his invention. But then it emerges that the technology has unintended consequences; users go cross-eyed. So the Steve Martin character winds up writing refund checks to everyone damaged by his invention.

That's how the Jerk came to terms with the damage he had wrought. That is not how the Zuck is doing it.

Faced with criticism from every quarter—including long-dead Supreme Court justices—over its practices, its opacity, its carelessness, its damage to privacy and public health, its rapaciousness, and its dishonesty, what did Facebook do? Well, it did three things:

1. It offered exactly the same rhetoric it has offered in a half dozen previous self-made scandals. "I'm sorry we didn't do more at the time," Zuckerberg wrote in a full-page newspaper ad. "I promise to do better for you." To evaluate that promise, may I call your attention to a college email exchange, quoted in a 2010 *Silicon Alley Insider* article and revisited by actual business insider Roger McNamee in his marvelous 2019 book *Zucked: Waking Up to the Facebook Catastrophe*:

    ZUCKERBERG: Yeah, so if you ever need info about anyone at Harvard, just ask. I have over 4,000 emails, pictures, SNS

FRIEND: What? How'd you manage that one?

ZUCKERBERG: People just submitted it. I don't know why. They "trust me." Dumb fucks.

2. It announced plans to empanel a forty-member Oversight Board for Content Decisions—a supposedly independent review board Facebook claims will be empowered to overturn decisions of management. Uh-huh.
3. It hired GOP public relations firms to deflect anger toward other tech giants, and to question the independence of activist groups mounting Facebook protests. The opposition researchers—using tactics plucked from the political-smear handbook—encouraged the press to explore those groups' connection to Jewish financeer George Soros. (He, of course, is already a boogeyman of the alt-right and constant target of anti-Semitic conspiracy theories and slanders.)

This is called scapegoating, conduct bespeaking a sense of ungodly arrogance and impunity, and no wonder. This is a company with 2.2 billion users worldwide and a 2018 profit of $27 billion. And its reach goes far beyond that. Facebook is in our computers, in our phones, in our transactions, in our communications, in our photo albums, and, to a chilling degree, in our heads. As Franklin Foer, author of *World Without Mind*, told Kara Swisher in her *Recode* podcast, "Our data is this cartography of the inside of our psyche. They know our weaknesses, and they know the things that give us pleasure and the things that cause us anxiety and anger. They use that information in order to keep us addicted. That makes the companies the enemies of independent thought."

Facebook and the other social media platforms, he said, are "the monopolists of mind."

That is not metaphor or hyperbole or some other glib figure of speech. It is biochemistry.

You may recall the uproar when journalists revealed that in 2012 Facebook employed A/B testing in users' News Feeds comparing degree of engagement to "positive" and "negative" content—testing that Facebook data scientists ultimately published as a 2014 paper in *Proceedings of the National Academy of Sciences* titled "Experimental evidence of massive-scale emotional contagion through social networks."

> We show, via a massive (N = 689,003) experiment on Facebook, that emotional states can be transferred to others via emotional contagion, leading people to experience the same emotions without their awareness. . . . More importantly, given the massive scale of social networks such as Facebook, even small effects can have large aggregated consequences: For example, the well-documented connection between emotions and physical well-being suggests the importance of these findings for public health. Online messages influence our experience of emotions, which may affect a variety of offline behaviors. And after all, an effect size of d = 0.001 at Facebook's scale is not negligible.

The monopolies of the mind—manipulated by opening and closing the taps of the neurotransmitter dopamine—is a frightening notion. From Foer's mouth it was also a cri de coeur, equal parts allegation and expression of despair. But it also suggests a path forward, because, after all, we know what we do with monopolies. We break them up. Which is precisely what a growing number of law professors, economists, political scientists, and economic-justice warriors wish to do.

"It is time to use antitrust again," says former labor secretary Robert Reich. "We should break up the hi-tech behemoths, or at least require they make their proprietary technology and data publicly available and share their platforms with smaller competitors."

Because it's not just anti-competitiveness and excessive market power we're talking about; "mind monopoly" is an enslavement scenario seemingly plucked from science fiction. So suggested Columbia Law School professor Tim Wu, author of *The Curse of Bigness: Antitrust in the New Gilded Age*, at a gathering hosted by *The Nation*. "I'm not worried about conquest by robots—we've already been conquered by inhuman creatures."

Can we be freed from their unearthly grip?

Obviously, there is plenty of precedent here. In 1902, the swashbuckling progressive president Teddy Roosevelt famously used the 1890 Sherman Antitrust Act to dismantle the predatory and nearly omnipotent Northern Securities Company, an all-consuming railroad holding company financed by J. P. Morgan and John D. Rockefeller. In 1906, he went after Standard Oil in federal court and won, eventually yielding a breakup of that voracious monopoly into thirty-four parts. Quoth the famed trustbuster: "The great corporations which we have grown to speak of rather loosely as trusts are the creatures of the State, and the State not only has the right to control them, but it is duty bound to control them wherever the need of such control is shown."

The intellectual underpinnings for antitrust enforcement in the era were largely constructed by the aforementioned progressive icon (and eventual Supreme Court justice) Louis Brandeis, who in 1912 asked the New York Economic Club, "What does democracy involve? Not merely political and religious liberty, but industrial liberty also." Brandeis feared the concentration of economic power as a threat to democracy itself. Absent government intervention, he said, "there is a power in this country of a few men so great as to be supreme over the law." That principle, and legal doctrine, held sway for decades—until the 1970s and the emergence of Milton Friedman and his Chicago school of economics. This deregulatory, laissez-faire philosophy saw intervention necessary only to protect "consumer welfare"—mainly by keeping monopolies from setting excessively high prices. And with the notable exception of the forced breakup of AT&T in the 1980s, the pricing standard had held sway ever since.

"Just being very big is not an antitrust violation," said Wharton School professor Herbert Hovenkamp, author of the twenty-one-volume *Antitrust Law: An Analysis of Antitrust Principles and Their Application*, to MarketWatch columnist Herbert Gold. "As long as firms are acting on their own [and] they're not conspiring with others, there hasn't been a great deal of room for antitrust intervention."

But here's the problem. The dollar-and-cent cost to the user of Facebook's offerings is zero, which is one of the best price points ever. Under existing antitrust doctrine, about forty years of precedent gives government little in the way of grounds for intervention. And there are no lawyers at the Federal Trade Commission calculating the value of the data we surrender as a quid pro quo for free services, let alone the question of how info-slavery and "welfare" even fit in the same sentence. As Carnegie Mellon professor of information technology Alessandro Acquisti told me, because our time, attention, and information are immediately monetized by the platform for ad sales, "Collectively, as consumers, we are paying the bills with hard cash from our pockets." But "It's almost a three-card monte game which obfuscates what was before [in the analog days] transparent."

Which is why activists like Denise Hearn, coauthor of *The Myth of Capitalism: Monopolies and the Death of Competition*, believe the legal status quo is woefully ill-suited to the modern excesses of Silicon Valley. "Our antitrust hardware and software are both in great need of updating to deal with the incredible amassed power of today's tech firms," she writes. "The consumer welfare standard that has been adopted for antitrust enforcement is completely ineffectual in dealing with our current realities. It's time to move our consumer welfare standard to the trash and reboot."

Indeed, a whole new school of antitrust law is coalescing around this idea. Called the Hipster Antitrust movement, and sometimes the New Brandeis movement, it focuses on other aspects of economic welfare, such as wage stagnation, income disparity, and unemployment. No reason "monopoly of the mind" can't be in there, too. A pioneer in the movement is economist Lina M. Khan, who looked at Amazon and its zillions of satisfied customers to imagine how they are, in the long run, being harmed by the company's dominance in retail and web services. In a research "note" titled "Amazon's Antitrust Paradox," she argues that low prices and great customer service paper over the potential—even the inevitability—of predatory pricing and anti-competitive conduct.

> This Note argues that the current framework in antitrust—specifically its pegging competition to "consumer welfare," defined as short-term price effects—is unequipped to capture the architecture of market power in the modern economy. We cannot

cognize the potential harms to competition posed by Amazon's dominance if we measure competition primarily through price and output. . . . The Note closes by considering two potential regimes for addressing Amazon's power: restoring traditional antitrust and competition policy principles or applying common carrier obligations and duties.

Khan focused on Amazon, but the same argument applies to the duopoly and, sure enough, things are brewing. Sen. Amy Klobuchar (D-Minnesota) has sponsored S.1812, the proposed Consolidation Prevention and Competition Promotion Act of 2017, which would essentially ban acquisitions by tech giants. A policy paper drafted by Sen. Mark Warner (D-Virginia) imagines mandating data transparency, data portability, and platform interoperability (among other measures) that would fracture the hegemony of the duopoly over their users and advertising markets—measures antithetical to their current business models. The issue is, as they say, gaining traction. Even since this chapter was first set in type, the question of antitrust enforcement has drifted from academic hypothesis to center stage of presidential politics. By June 2019, led by Sen. Elizabeth Warren, seven of the announced candidates for the Democratic presidential nomination had endorsed or were contemplating a forced breakup or imposition of regulation. And this is not necessarily a partisan enterprise. Sen. Orrin Hatch (R-Utah) in August 2018 wrote to FTC chairman Joseph Simons asking for an investigation into Google's data-collection and search practices. Hatch cited "disquieting" reports about censorship and partisan bias, presumably the specious Trump complaints about systematic mistreatment of Republicans. But however imaginary those allegations are, the chairman of the

Senate Finance Committee is not someone a company wishes to be disquieted.

Among those on the interventionist bandwagon is Harold Feld, senior vice president of Public Knowledge, the public-interest group advocating an open internet and access to tools of communication. In a 2018 blog post he wrote, "When platforms have become so central to our lives that a change in algorithm can dramatically crash third-party businesses, when social media plays such an important role in our lives that entire businesses exist to pump up your follower numbers, and when a multi-billion dollar industry exists for the sole purpose of helping businesses game search engine rankings, lawmakers need to stop talking hopefully about self-regulation and start putting in place enforceable rights to protect the public interest."

Feld, however, is under no illusions. Demanding responsible citizenship from corporations, he wrote, "usually works about as well as Canute ordering back the tide." Breaking up Facebook would not by regulatory fiat solve the filter-bubble problems, or the privacy problem, or the advertising-market problem. Most likely, he concluded, it would simply create a cluster of smaller players with precisely the same practices. Recall that the AT&T Corporation breakup yielded so-called Baby Bells, most of which eventually reconsolidated into such little telecom boutiques as Verizon and AT&T Inc. Not only is antitrust not a panacea, it would also disrupt the very features of these valuable utilities we truly love and have come to expect as our due.

So, then, how to smartly, effectively, rationally, safely break the fuckers up?

Answer: Let them, under the threat of government regulation and litigation, do it themselves. Facebook's and Google's best chance to forge a future on their own terms is to preemptively alter business practices—even to some extent their business models—to assuage critics and government watchdogs here and in Europe. In other words: to negotiate the terms of their surrender. Think of Germany after World War I. The Versailles Treaty was harsh, punitive, and utterly humiliating. How different the twentieth century would have been had the kaiser sued for peace in 1917 under terms of partial disarmament.

This is what we need: partial disarmament—from data and privacy abuses, from opacity, from brutish marketplace behavior, from the neutralization of potential competition by acquisition. As columnist Joe Nocera wrote for Bloomberg, "It's true that the government failed to break up IBM Corp. or Microsoft Corp. Even so, the mere fact of the lawsuits changed the behavior of the companies, allowing for innovation and competition that the two monopolies had prevented. The software industry came about in no small part because IBM didn't dare try to stop it; Google was able to grow knowing that Microsoft wouldn't try to harm it the way it had Netscape." Furthermore, recall again the breakup of AT&T. In 1982, the value of that company was $47.5 billion. Today, Verizon and AT&T Inc., only two of the seven reconstituted Baby Bells, are worth $479 billion. The whole is sometimes far less than the sum of its parts. Are you paying attention, Mark Zuckerberg?

And while you're looking over your shoulder, consider threats not from regulators or litigators or legislators, but from competitors. No less a personage than Tim Berners-Lee, the founder of the internet, has launched a company called Inrupt, which aims to overturn the data economy by wresting control of user data from the duopoly and others and vastly decentralizing it into the control of individuals. Using open-source software called Solid—also launched by

Berners-Lee—developers worldwide can create apps that offer the same utility of the dominant ones, but which keep personal data private and within user control. Needless to say, this would play havoc with Facebook's business model. Your data is at the heart of its algorithm and its ad targeting. Which, as Berners-Lee told *Fast Company* magazine in the fall of 2018, is just hard cheese: "We are not talking to Facebook and Google about whether or not to introduce a complete change where all their business models are completely upended overnight," he said. "We are not asking their permission."

What does radical reform look like? In *Zucked*, early Facebook investor and advisor turned activist critic Roger McNamee offers some suggestions:

1. Allowing users to switch off the filter-bubble part of the EdgeRank algorithm.
2. Intuitive and frictionless user control of their own data.
3. The ability to port one's own "social graph"—collection of friends and followers—from platform to platform.
4. Designating tech platforms as "fiduciaries," required like bankers and stockbrokers to put their customers' interest ahead of their own.
5. The embrace of "human-driven technology," obliging tech companies to account for unintended consequences, whether cross-eyed glasses wearers or addicted teenagers or election tampering.

I would add three more:

6. Forced divestiture of Instagram and WhatsApp, and prohibition of further "horizontal" acquisitions.

7. Spin off the ad-services function from the Facebook content platform, eradicating the corrupt incentive to promote "engagement" at all costs.
8. Creation of an Internet Product Safety Commission, with the power to regulate the social media giants. This would include the power to audit the governing algorithms, mandate robust content moderation, and perhaps even (borrowing from public health quarantines and automobile speed limits) prevent viral contamination by capping to sub-geometric levels users' capacity to share.

In sum, the duopoly has a choice. Perhaps it is a Hobson's choice, because the antitrust alternative is too risky. But there it is nonetheless: radical reform—for the benefit of society and very likely their own shareholders—or Versailles.

Not that we should be naïve. Having witnessed Facebook's history of arrogant unilateralism—and the Republican cult of deregulation, especially under Trump—any rational observer would be forgiven for snorting sardonically at any real-life prospects for McNamee's prescription. But undeniably the pressure is on, and there is evidence that Zuckerberg himself is seeing the handwriting on the touchscreen. At the end of March 2019, he posted a memo to the world at least purporting to embrace some level of government intervention:

I believe Facebook has a responsibility to help address these issues, and I'm looking forward to discussing them with lawmakers around the world. We've built advanced systems for finding harmful content, stopping election interference and making ads more transparent. But people shouldn't have to rely on individual companies addressing these issues by themselves. We should have a broader debate about what we want as a society and how regulation can help. These four areas are important, but, of course, there's more to discuss.

The rules governing the Internet allowed a generation of entrepreneurs to build services that changed the world and created a lot of value in people's lives. It's time to update these rules to define clear responsibilities for people, companies and governments going forward.

The history of Facebook, of course, is the history of conciliatory Zuckerberg rhetoric followed by arrogant business as usual. But the history of rapid social and political change is the history of individual citizens sensing and exploiting opportunity. In the space of a few years, for example, same-sex marriage went from a scare tactic of the George W. Bush reelection campaign to law of the land.

When it comes to taming the duopoly, it falls on the electorate—it falls on you—to engineer the same lightning transformation. To see the daylight and seize the day.

9

Boycott

For the purposes of this argument, we shall not assume that the right-wing media are just a mirror image of the so-called mainstream media. We shall not assume that, because, in fact, the right-wing media are *not* just a mirror image of the so-called mainstream media. I shall demonstrate this presently, but first, let us think about the fundamental beneath that fundamental disparity:

Is there a liberal bias in mainstream media?

Yes. And, also, no.

In the Venn diagram of values, journalism and liberalism do have a huge overlap. Questioning authority, suspicion of big money, "reform" in general, afflicting the comfortable and comforting the afflicted—which is really another way of saying "social justice." Journalism isn't a political party, much less an "opposition party," but as a constitutionally protected watchdog, it is inherently adversarial to, or at least skeptical of, the sitting government. (Ask Barack Obama.

On the Media, just for instance, repeatedly assailed Obama for his drone policy, his lack of transparency, his Justice Department's prosecution of journalists, his Defense Department's onerous laws of war revisions, and his historic inaccessibility to the press.)

Journalistic attitudes have been called a "sensibility," versus an ideology or doctrine, which is about right. On the other hand, while the latest survey numbers are a bit outdated, in 2013 only 7 percent of journalists self-identified as Republican. (Fifty-two percent identified as independent.) So the sensibility is not a figment of the right's imagination, and as the collapse of the media economy kills journalism jobs across the heartland, the coastal (i.e., blue-state) concentration of the media business becomes more pronounced.

But does that prove political bias? No, it does not.

With some notable and horrifying exceptions, large news organizations—especially the ones dismissed as hubs of liberal bias—are rigorous in their work. The protocols of large news organizations police fairness and accuracy and are difficult to circumvent within a newsroom. When a story is deemed particularly likely to be politically damaging, the caution is even greater. (Indeed, here the press tends toward a more insidious sin of false balance.) Nonetheless, when things happen, we report them, and when bad things happen, we report them louder. That is not evidence of bias. It is evidence of observation and judgment.

For crying out loud, if a baseball player strikes out six times in a game, the press will say so and nobody will allege bias. If we describe a devastating hurricane a "killer storm"—because it has taken lives—we aren't accused of having an "anti-weather agenda." Yet when we identify lies, failed policies, violations of the law in a political or governmental context, it's seen as a smoking gun of bias and partisanship. At long last, how is this not clear? There is a difference between reporting and polemic. What we are biased against is calamity, abuse, dishonesty, failure, and wrongdoing.

Has the press piled on Donald Trump? Of course it has. But no matter what Sean Hannity tells you, this is not the smoking gun of anti-Republican bias. It is simply an eyewitness account of historic depravity. As comedian John Mulaney puts it, "There's a horse loose in a hospital." We're just following it around, incredulously, assessing the damage. So if it isn't too hard to keep two ideas in your head simultaneously, yes, the press is liberal in its sensibilities and also the Trump administration is a shit show. If you dismiss rigorous, evidence-based reporting as proof of partisanship, well, we've located the bias, haven't we?

In fact, here is a little experiment. If you believe the press has a partisan bias against Trump, please offer five examples (out of hundreds of thousands of stories written during his administration) that support your suspicions. Let's call it the Integrity Test. Only two ground rules: You must demonstrate their falsity (or even implausibility) and must show that any errors in fact or assumption were not immediately corrected by the news organization when they came to light. You may even use the explicitly lefty media, such as Salon and *Mother Jones*, to build your case. There is no time limit.

Good luck. You'll need it.

Now then, can we say the same about the right-wing media? Can we say they have a conservative sensibility, but are nonpartisan and rigorous in their reporting?

O, the mirth! No, we cannot. I am not speaking of the *National Review*, or the (defunct) *Weekly Standard* (which lost its arch-conservative sugar daddy and shut down for the crime of being too critical of Trump), or *Commentary*, or the *Hill*, which certainly fit that description. I'm speaking of Breitbart News, TheBlaze, Rush

Limbaugh, Mark Levin, the *Daily Caller,* Newsmax, and, most dangerously, Fox News Channel—which, except for some midday straight-news programming—is not journalism at all, but rather propaganda, opposition research, and demagoguery with no professional standards of rigor, accuracy, or fairness. It is, in a word, vile. Allow me to apply the Integrity Test.

- June 2007. *Fox & Friends* host calls Mr. Rogers an "evil, evil man" for creating an entitled generation of children by telling them they are "special."
- June 2008. Fox host shows image of the Obamas' celebratory fist-bumping, and host E. D. Hill says, "A fist bump? A pound? A terrorist fist jab?"
- July 2008. *Fox & Friends* airs doctored images of two *New York Times* reporters, Photoshopped to make them appear like ghouls.
- July 2009. Glenn Beck calls Obama a racist. "I'm not saying that he doesn't like white people. I'm saying he has a problem. He has a—this guy is, I believe, a racist."
- July 2009. Beck accuses John Holdren, director of the White House Office of Science and Technology Policy, of plans for "forcing abortions and putting sterilants in the drinking water to control population."
- May 2011. *Fox & Friends* host Brian Kilmeade on American's lack of ethnic purity: "We keep marrying other species and other ethnicities . . . Swedes have pure genes . . . in America we marry everybody."
- May 2012. *Fox & Friends* airs four-minute video attack of Obama in the form of a campaign ad—produced by Fox.
- March 2013. Commentator Ann Coulter says, "I used to

think women should not be able to vote and now I think liberal women should not be able to hold office."

- July 2013. Anchor Lauren Green asks religion scholar Reza Aslan how a Muslim could write a historical book about Jesus: "Why would you be interested in the founder of Christianity?"

- September 2013. Bill O'Reilly blames a slain black teenager for his own shooting death: "If Trayvon Martin had been wearing a jacket like you are and a tie . . . I don't think George Zimmerman would've had any problem. But he was wearing a hoodie, and he looked a certain way, and that way is how gangstas look."

- May 2017. Parroting a FoxNews.com article (later retracted), Newt Gingrich alleges the street murder of Seth Rich, a Democratic National Committee staffer, "was apparently an assassination" and blames Rich—not Russian hackers—for leaked DNC emails.

- February 2018. Mike Huckabee on the Parkland high school shooting: "We have systematically removed God from our schools. Should we be so surprised that schools would become a place of carnage?"

In October 2009, Glenn Beck said, "Forty-five percent of doctors 'say they'll quit' if health care reform passes." False. In April 2010, faced with an accusation of fearmongering, Bill O'Reilly said, "We researched to find out if anybody on Fox News had ever said you're going to jail if you don't buy health insurance. Nobody's ever said it." False about falsity. The jail lie had been aired on Fox four times. In November 2013, Dana Perino said, "The insurance industry is actually run by mostly Democrats." False. In April 2014,

Todd Starnes said, "Liberals have figured out a Facebook algorithm and all the people getting banned from Facebook are somehow conservatives." False. In June 2014, Jeanine Pirro said ISIS leader Abu Bakr al-Baghdadi was "released by Obama in 2009." False. In August 2014, Tucker Carlson said, "Far more children died last year drowning in their bathtubs than were killed accidentally by guns." False. In June 2015, Steve Doocy said, "NASA scientists fudged the numbers to make 1998 the hottest year to overstate the extent of global warming." False. In June 2015, Gavin McInnes (whose Proud Boys racist gang was charged over a 2018 New York brawl and who was subsequently kicked off TheBlaze and YouTube for hate speech) said, "Fifty percent of murders in Texas have been linked to illegal aliens." False. In September 2015, Eric Bolling said, "In countries where there are higher, more strict gun laws, there is more gun violence." False. In November 2018, Lou Dobbs said, "We are watching, you know, millions of illegal immigrants cross our borders, and many of them voting in the past election that's what, just a couple weeks ago." False.

All of the above, of course, is not merely a conservative viewpoint but partisan rhetoric in line with the talking points of the Republican Party. No surprise there. In 2010, Media Matters for America—a liberal watchdog group that monitors right-wing media—released a leaked 2009 Fox management memo instructing producers to avoid the term "public option" in discussing a key provision of Obamacare, but rather "government option" or "government-run health insurance"—in accordance with the GOP's Big-Government-socialized-medicine rhetoric. A subsequent Fox memo mandated that reporters qualify all climate-science reporting as follows: "theories are based upon data that critics have called into question." Called into question by politicians and the right-wing media, not by scientists. Meantime, Fox has been repeatedly caught in the act of dishonest video editing—in two cases to exaggerate crowd sizes at events for Republican politicians Sarah Palin and Michele Bachmann. Host Sean Hannity twice selectively edited videotape of Barack Obama to mislead viewers, showing the president saying, "Taxes are scheduled to go up substantially next year, for everybody." Hannity called this "a rare moment of honesty." But he had cut out the first clause of Obama's statement: "*Under the tax plan passed by the last administration,* taxes are scheduled to go up substantially next year, for everybody."

This is the man who proudly took the stage with Donald Trump at a Missouri political rally, having been introduced by the president as one of the media personalities who has "done an incredible job for us." Scanning the hall, Hannity gestured to the press corps and told the crowd, "By the way, all those people in the back are fake news."

Demonizing the free press. Denying science and other objective facts. Manipulating images. Pumping up conspiracy theories and supposed "scandals" (Benghazi, Fast and Furious, the Seth Rich murder) that weren't. Active collaboration with a political party. Racism. Countless lies and hate speech. Fomenting rage about a supposed sinister deep state. As I said: vile. But what to do about that? There is not only a market for this kind of poison, there is a bull market for it. While the rest of the media economy is gasping for air, Fox News Channel approached $2 billion in profits in 2018. Lovers of truth cannot wish that away because the audience needs its fix. Fox has the same business model as the Sinaloa Cartel.

But if the audience feeds on righteous resentment, Fox lives on billions of advertiser dollars. What if those advertisers found it disadvantageous, for reasons of reputation, to continue spending money there? What if they faced a boycott? Let us consider.

There are two questions here. One concerns the wisdom of such a thing, and the other concerns effectiveness. I'll begin with the second issue.

An oft-cited 2012 study on the subject, by Paul Sergius Koku of Florida Atlantic University, came to the following conclusion: "The results show that consumer boycotts launched by individuals on the internet are ineffective in inflicting economic harm on the targeted firm." If you were, say, the *Ethical Consumer*, that would be a bit of a buzzkill. As of the first week of January 2019, that nonprofit British monitor of ethical corporate and governmental conduct was pressing no fewer than forty boycotts for a host of perceived ethical transgressions. This includes Ben & Jerry's, for having an Israeli subsidiary that sells ice cream in the Occupied Territories (but not, FYI, any companies doing business in Russia, Turkey, Philippines, China, Myanmar, Venezuela, Zimbabwe, Nicaragua, Cuba, Poland, or other major violators of human rights); the British dog-show TV program *Crufts*, for celebrating dog breeding; the academic publisher Elsevier for charging too much, and for its activism against copyright piracy; Method cleaning products, for being owned by SC Johnson, some of whose other brands test products on animals; and Starbucks, for belonging to the Grocery Manufacturers Association, which filed suit against Vermont over a GMO-labeling statute.

Putting aside the hair-trigger sanctimony behind the group's activities, please note that none of the targets is exactly teetering on the edge.

On the other hand, some boycotts have played havoc with the targets. The state of Arizona passed an anti-immigration law with the anodyne title "The Support Our Law Enforcement and Safe

Neighborhoods Act." The law, among other harsh measures, essentially legalized racial profiling and—before it was struck down in federal court—led to a boycott of the state, costing Arizona an estimated $45 million in conference business. When North Carolina's 2016 Public Facilities Privacy & Security Act explicitly removed discrimination protections for LGBT citizens, a national boycott devastated the economy in the sports, entertainment, conference, and tourism sectors and cost the state tens of millions of dollars in direct spending, hundreds of millions in corporate investments, and thousands of jobs. The Associated Press projected the twelve-year loss to the state at $3.76 billion. Soon thereafter, the law was repealed and replaced.

When Apple faced a boycott for labor abuses by its Chinese subcontractor Foxconn, the company immediately cleaned up its supply chain, as did Nike before it. A 1996 *Harvard Business Review* case study of a Greenpeace campaign against Shell over a North Sea environmental issue estimated Shell's sales in Germany to have dropped 40 percent.

That statistic is courtesy of Northwestern University professor Daniel Diermeier, author of *Reputation Rules: Strategies for Building Your Company's Most Valuable Asset.* If customers care passionately about an issue, if their sacrifice is small, if the underlying issue is easy to understand, and if the media follow closely, Diermeier says, boycotts can change behavior.

Writing in the December 1986 *Journal of Consumer Policy,* Stephen W. Pruitt and Monroe Friedman studied the effect of twenty-one consumer boycotts on public corporations: "A major finding of the study was that consumer boycott announcements were followed by statistically significant decreases in stock prices for the target firms. In addition, the overall market value of the target firms dropped by an average of more than $120 million over the two-month post-announcement period."

Because reputation has value. On balance sheets, it is calculated as an asset called "goodwill." Which is better than badwill.

In December 2018, Bloomberg reported that the conservative zealots and financiers of both Breitbart News and (defunct) Cambridge Analytica, hedge fund founder Robert Mercer and his daughter Rebekah, dramatically pulled back on their investments in hard-right candidates and causes under pressure from such liberal activists as Sleeping Giants. This included protests at Mercer's home, pressure on university endowments to withdraw investments in Mercer's fund, and an attempt to get Rebekah Mercer dropped from the American Museum of Natural History board.

Even as the Bloomberg scoop broke, Fox News Channel was facing some bad will of its own. Prime-time host Tucker Carlson, who had flirted with racist sentiments and borderline hate speech for two years, finally broke the camel's back with his allegation that immigrants make the country "poorer and dirtier and more divided." This triggered an immediate boycott of his program's advertisers, and such brands as Pacific Life, Bowflex, Land Rover, SanDisk, IHOP, and Just For Men pulled their ad schedules. (Just a few months later, in March 2019, the Fox hunters at Media Matters unearthed radio conversations Carlson had with shock jock Bubba the Love Sponge in which he amused drive-timers with vulgar misogyny, including musing about sex with underage girls, homophobia ("faggot"), and naked racism. Iraqis, he said, are "semiliterate primitive monkeys.")

The Carlson advertiser exodus was reminiscent of previous campaigns that drove Fox's Bill O'Reilly (2017) and Glenn Beck (2011) off the air, even if it was a bit of three-card monte, with those offended advertisers mainly just moving their ads to other Fox shows—and even if those vacuums were filled by the equally toxic Laura Ingraham, Sean Hannity, and Jeanne Pirro. (In March 2019, Pirro herself was suspended for two weeks after questioning the loyalty of U.S. Rep. Ilhan Omar, a practicing Muslim. "Is her adherence to this Islamic doctrine indicative of her adherence to Sharia law," Pirro asked, rhetorically, on the air, "which in itself is antithetical to the United States Constitution?") With the once (relatively) safe prime-time harbors getting ever more treacherous, it raises the question: Could a boycott of sufficient scale be waged against the entire channel for its totality of bad faith, hate speech, propaganda, and damage to our democracy? Can a campaign cleave to Professor Diermeier's four checklist items to scare advertisers away from Fox altogether?

Dishonesty hasn't seemed to be sufficient cause. Nor partisanship. Nor even hatefulness. But there is one sin that no advertiser can risk being associated with. The channel that wraps itself in the American flag is unpatriotic. It is against truth, it is against justice for all, it is against the Statue of Liberty, it is against the Bill of Rights (with the exception of the Second Amendment, which it *lurrrrrvs*), and it has constantly agitated against the investigation into a foreign adversary's subversion of our most fundamental expression of democracy: the election.

Marketers are obsessive stewards of what they call "brand safety," which means protecting brands from negative consumer judgment when ads appear adjacent to controversial or objectionable content, such as violence, sex, drugs, crime, and terrorism. Because of computerized "programmatic" ad buys online, those unfortunate ad placements can happen accidentally, but for at least a century advertisers in analog media have been cautious about the so-called editorial environment. Here's ad-tech consultant Scott Cunningham, writing for the Brand Safety Institute, who observes that even audience growth for provocative content can come back to haunt brands: "Ironically, marketers and buyers interviewed understand that this type of placement might lead to better conversion results. However, the potential reputational damage to the Brand caused by associating with some content might also lead to devaluation of the brand in the long term." Brand awareness is nice, and worth paying for, but please note: Charles Manson has fantastic brand awareness. So does Benedict Arnold. And smallpox.

Long term, can any brand stomach being associated with an un-American hate machine?

No, which argues for a boycott of Fox, the *Daily Caller*, Breitbart News, the *Washington Examiner*, et al.—not for being partisan supporters but for abusing First Amendment privileges to be organs of the corrupt state. Just for instance, on the last day of 2018, the *Examiner* ran a story with this headline: "MAGA list: 205 'historic results' help Trump make case for 2020 re-election." Sure enough, writer Paul Bedard lists all of the administration's great achievements. A careless reader might miss the disclaimer: "the following list was compiled by the White House." Yes, the *Examiner* uncritically printed the Trump's-eye-view of his first two years in office. And you know who was *dee*-lighted? #RealDonaldTrump! On New Year's Day, in the midst of a government shutdown, he tweeted about this journalistic confirmation of his many triumphs.

> "Washington Examiner – 'MAGA list: 205 'historic results' help Trump make case for 2020 re-election.' True!"

But that brings us back to the first question I posed: Would it be wise? Hmm. There is a very compelling argument for "No, it would be unwise, and maybe itself antithetical to democratic freedoms."

There is, first of all, the question of free speech. It is axiomatic in First Amendment circles that the treatment for ugly speech is not less speech, but more—to overwhelm ignorance with reason, bile with respect, misinformation with truth. That's why in 1978, the ACLU supported American Nazis' right to march in Skokie, Illinois, then an enclave of Holocaust survivors. Political speech, however inflammatory or repugnant, is too precious for the government to suppress. Moreover, the idea of censoring ideas, however baseless or cruel those ideas may be, is a slippery slope. Think about the 2017 Public Theater production of *Julius Caesar*, which lost its sponsors after a Breitbart News article complained that the Caesar-as-Trump title character (spoiler alert) is assassinated. Fox picked up on it, and Donald Jr. started tweeting, and all hell broke loose. Delta Airlines pulled its Public Theater funding altogether, stating that the play "does not reflect Delta Airlines' values"—as if in 1599 Shakespeare had been promoting political violence. (Read the play. It's the opposite. It's a tragedy.)

Another example was Gamergate, the proto-alt-right protest discussed in chapter 3. When in 2014 the (now defunct) *Gawker* covered the story in a way that (by reporting accurately) displeased the angry gamers, the angry subjects launched a boycott of *Gawker*'s advertisers, reportedly costing the publication in excess of $1 million. We don't permit censorship by the government; shall we encourage it from the mob?

Indeed, the First Amendment applies only to government suppression of speech; there is no legal requirement for media or business to accept "anything goes." On the contrary, the aforementioned "jaws of consent"—also known as the Overton window—has long been a measure of society's tolerance (or intolerance) for extremes. Media, in fact, have always been expected to be responsible gatekeepers, respectful of the sensibilities of the majorities of their audiences. But please recall: Ben Bagdikian did not fear for democracy because the media played that role too haphazardly; he feared that they played that role too hegemonically and too well.

To media critic Jack Shafer, this is an easy call. "This is dangerous," he wrote in 2017 when a boycott got Fox's Bill O'Reilly thrown off the air. "The last thing I want is a mediasphere in which advertisers regain the power to determine what is acceptable fare and what is not."

Not only does Shafer not see advertisers as trustworthy arbiters of journalistic standards, "The expectation that advertisements equal approval of an anchor or commentator's conduct, be it on-screen or off, takes us to places I'd rather not visit." His solution: If you don't like Fox, change the channel.

Wait . . . what? When he gets to that conclusion, it all becomes so clear. He has missed the point. The issue is not personal taste in viewing, nor even personal politics. It is not about an episode or episodes of bad judgment or overreach; if it were, most every columnist, commentator, and comedian would have long since been given the heave-ho. With Fox, it is about a systematic, twenty-three-year-long effort to vilify and propagandize and delegitimize democratic institutions. It is "media" in the sense that it comes through your cable system and looks like a news channel. But it is not that; it is a political attack machine, amoral except when it is immoral, and the apotheosis of the very partisan bias it purports to balance. It is not part of the Fourth Estate. It is a fifth column of subversion of the institutions of our democracy. And as long as we're speaking of ordinal numbers, think about *The Third Man*, the post-WWII thriller about black marketeer Harry Lime, who trades in deadly, contaminated penicillin. The late mastermind of Fox, Roger Ailes, was Harry Lime. Sean Hannity is the bad penicillin.

I must be clear here. When the so-called liberal press finds fault with politicians or government, which is after all our constitutional role and what we do for a living, the reflexive attacks on our integrity and motives are sadly standard. We didn't document Nixon's crimes; oh, no, no, no, *we hated America*. We didn't uncover Pentagon lies about Vietnam; *we were spies and traitors*. We didn't cover Anita Hill's charges against Supreme Court nominee Clarence Thomas; *we ran a "high-tech lynching."* So how in the world can I so glibly throw around the word "subversion" for the act of criticizing people in power and institutions of government?

The answer is: evidence. Mountains of evidence piling up since 1996. "Dirty immigrants" and Sharia law and Democratic Party murders and Muslim Obama. It's all there, on tape, for any citizen and any advertiser to see.

Shall advertisers be the arbiters of patriotism? Why the hell not? As noted, under the rubric of "brand safety," they keep their distance from any controversy that can render long-term damage to their businesses. Isn't "vicious, destructive propaganda machine carrying water for a ruthless foreign adversary" as unsafe as can be?

This is not, in the end, a First Amendment question or even a strategic one. It comes down to simple right and wrong. Think about the granddaddy of all twentieth-century boycotts—a world-wide conspiracy of rejection against the apartheid society of South Africa, in the spheres not only of commerce, but also academia and sport. It took thirty-five years, but in the end the protest laid bare the very illegitimacy of the racist state.

The result was democracy.

10

How to Know if a Movie Sucks or if the Russians Are Trying to Trick You

Back in the day, to choose a movie, you looked at the listings in your local paper. They included basic information about theaters and running times, but they were surrounded by an eye-catching display of advertisements promoting the flicks screening in your area. These were miraculous ads, actually, because they all declared that the movie in question was a timeless blockbuster. If you were paying any attention at all, though, you knew which ones totally sucked.

To crack the code, you needed to know a few things, such as recognizing leading critics and credible sources among the names whose blurbs supposedly endorsed the film. "Heartbreaking and timeless" from Pauline Kael at *The New Yorker* was money in the bank. From Peter Travers at *Rolling Stone*, who never met a movie he didn't like, it was meaningless. From Fox 45 Albany, it was even meaninglesser.

You had to be aware of ellipses and other selective editing. Please note that "a bonanza of incompetence" can easily be shortened for blurb purposes to "A bonanza!" Likewise, "it was so thrilling after 105 turgid minutes to see the closing credits roll for this debacle that I cried tears of joy" can become "Thrilling! . . . Tears of joy!"

And it helped to know about the species of dubious journalists called "blurb whores." They work for some obscure medium and get press passes in exchange for their gushing quotes, which don't even need to be published, just filled out on a handy comment card after (or before) the movie is over. "Heartwarming masterpiece"—says guy nobody ever heard of, from bullshit website.

One of the biggest U.S. cinematic flops of the twentieth century, for example, was the Kevin Costner ego epic *Waterworld*. But not to Alan Frank (?) of the *Daily Star* (?): "SPLASH HIT!" his blurb incorrectly declared. "COSTNER PUTS ON OCEANS OF THRILLS . . . Spectacular entertainment—thrilling and suspenseful from start to finish. . . . Crammed with stunning stunts and rousing action . . . moviegoers will be getting great value for money." Moviegoers, maybe. Investors, unfortunately not.

An even bigger flop was the high-priced buddy flick *Ishtar*, starring Dustin Hoffman and Warren Beatty. It cost 51 million 1987 dollars to produce and pulled in $14.4 million at the box office. On Rotten Tomatoes, the movie has an aggregate rating of 34 percent from critics and 37 percent from civilians. One of the most generous reviews came from Janet Maslin of *The New York Times*, who concluded that *Ishtar* wasn't nearly as horrible as everyone was whispering. "It's a likable, good-humored hybrid, a mixture of small, funny moments and the pointless, oversized spectacle that these days is sine qua non for any hot-weather hit. The worst of it is painless; the best is funny, sly, cheerful, and, here and there, even genuinely inspired."

Not a pan, and not exactly a rave either. Here's what the movie ad said: "HOT WEATHER HIT."

The point here is not the vagaries of Hollywood film production. The point is media literacy. It really doesn't take much knowledge or scrutiny to divine the truth behind movie-ad hype, and it doesn't take much to evaluate what shows up on Facebook. And yet . . . fake news. These are some of the most widely shared headlines of the 2016 election campaign, every last one of them from a phony source:

"Pope Francis shocks world, endorses Donald Trump for president." This from WTOE 5, which may look like TV call letters, but is just a supposedly "satirical" website that made money when gullible people clicked on their bogus headlines.

"WikiLeaks confirms Hillary sold weapons to ISIS . . . Then drops another bombshell." This came from the ultra-partisan site the Political Insider ("Get breaking news alerts that the liberal media won't tell you"), based on the entirely unhidden fact that the U.S. government sold weapons to Qaddafi's Libya.

"FBI agent suspected in Hillary email leaks found dead in apparent murder-suicide." That fabrication was courtesy of the "*Denver Guardian*," which does not exist and has never existed.

"FBI director received millions from Clinton Foundation, his brother's law firm does Clinton's taxes." Completely invented by the fringe-right fake-news site called Ending the Fed News.

"ISIS leader calls for American Muslim voters to support Hillary Clinton." Another invented story, but another "satire" site, WNDR—which is also not a broadcast station of any kind.

What with the filter-bubble problems discussed throughout these pages, and the human nature that nourishes it, it's not hard to see how Hillary haters would discard common sense to feed on this preposterous clickbait. But lack of media sophistication—or even basic understanding—is by no means limited to angry partisans. It is endemic.

The second annual State of Critical Thinking study by the Massachusetts education-technology firm MindEdge presented 1,002 college students and professionals, aged eighteen to thirty, a series of nine articles and asked them to identify real news or fake. Of the group, 19 percent were able to get at least eight of nine answers correct. But 52 percent flunked, with between four and nine wrong answers.

A 2018 Pew Research Center study presented 5,035 subjects with five statements of facts and five statements of opinion and asked them to identify which were which. "A majority of Americans correctly identified at least three of the five statements in each set," the authors reported, "but this result is only a little better than random guesses. Far fewer Americans got all five correct, and roughly a quarter got most or all wrong."

A Stanford University study published in 2016 found that more than 80 percent of middle schoolers could not distinguish between genuine news and so-called native advertising—advertiser content dressed up to look like actual editorial—even when it bore the standard (tiny) label "Sponsored Content."

In the same study, a group of university students (including those at Stanford, which, the researchers ruefully observed, accepts only 6 percent of applicants) were shown Twitter messages from progressive organizations. Asked to evaluate them, fully a third of the subjects failed to consider how the organizations' political ideology might influence the assertions within the tweets. "Overall," the authors concluded, "young people's ability to reason about information on the Internet can be summed up in one word: bleak. Our 'digital natives' may be able to flit between Facebook and Twitter while simultaneously uploading a selfie to Instagram and texting a friend. But when it comes to evaluating information that flows around social media channels, they are easily duped."

This is what is known as media illiteracy, and it's a problem.

It's actually a weird problem, because, as dismally documented in chapter 6, hardly anybody trusts the press and imputes to it all kinds of evils—but, by and large, they identify all the wrong evils. At *On the Media*, we document errors of omission and commission, chronic and acute, on a weekly basis. They are plentiful enough to have produced a thousand-plus hours of *OTM* programming over twenty years. Yet, as inveterate, professional pointers of fingers, we're faced constantly with the reality that the prevailing public criticism of the media misses the actual failures and obsesses over imaginary ones. This social media post pretty well sums up the prevailing narrative:

Frederico Romano
May 17, 2018

The very first misconception is that the MSM (news) knows what the hell they're talking about . . . the "news" today is nothing more than a conduit for the left to spew its mantra by spinning most stories with a hearty slice of liberal politics/policies.

Thing is, Frederico, just for starters, there is no "the news." Remember, please, that "the media" is a plural. We are not speaking of a monolith, but rather a sector composed of thousands of so-called mainstream outlets and countless more blogs, websites, YouTube channels, and so on. And they are by and large in competition with one another. They are not a cabal. They do not talk among themselves. They do not owe allegiance to any third party. There is no secret handshake.

As noted above, there are surely institutional tendencies—a sensibility—that invites suspicions (or, in the case of Frederico and many others, certainty) of political bias. And indeed there are biases, but they aren't especially political. There is a bias, for instance, toward conventional wisdom, a.k.a. groupthink. There is a bias toward drama. There is a bias toward being first with information, whether especially relevant and important or not. And, of course, there is the bias toward exposing hypocrisy, malfeasance, scoundrels, foolishness, and lies. Because that is what watchdogs do. Also, per "drama" above, who don't love that shit? (Watergate was a scandal and a crisis, but ... oo la la!)

So, then, how to help Americans understand where the real problems lie, and how to evaluate the likely merits of the incendiary story Uncle Jack has posted on Facebook? How to promote at least the most rudimentary level of critical thinking? Surely there is no shortage of folks giving it a shot.

There is the National Leadership Conference on Media Literacy, Center for Media Literacy, Common Sense Education, the National Association for Media Literacy Education, Media Education Foundation, the News Literacy Project, Media Literacy Now, Center for Social Media, and a whole mess of other organizations who have developed excellent programs, apps, and K–12 curricula with the common goal of helping Americans—especially young Americans—navigate treacherous and sometimes uncharted seas of information.

And how are they doing, as a group? Well, obviously, they are doing terribly—so terribly that Sen. Mark Warner (D-Virginia) has floated federal intervention via the funding of media-literacy programs. It's a swell idea, except that the problem is not a shortage of media-literacy programs; those groups I listed have among them produced a vast body of work. The problem is actual time spent with the information. As social studies and communications curricula shrink nationwide—replaced by all STEM all the time, and the constant standardized testing that goes with it—American students get at best a glancing exposure to the media-literacy basics.

As far back as 2011, writing in the journal *Action in Teacher Education*, professor Vanessa Greenwood of Montclair State University recognized the lopsided emphasis on technology education:

> Although P12 schools cope with the chronic top-down push to achieve technological proficiency by the eighth grade, there simultaneously exists a bottom-up need to address specific challenges among young people, including (1) unequal access to a participatory culture (for which technological proficiency is prerequisite), (2) lack of transparency in the ways media shape young people's perception of the world, and (3) the ethical challenges of preparing young people for their increasingly public roles as media producers. . . . Media literacy education reconciles the clash between the standardized bureaucracy of technology education and the democratic implications of empowering youth as participatory citizens through their active and public uses of technology.

If only. We saw in the Stanford study how poorly equipped our next generation of leaders is merely to parse their own Twitter feeds. This is alarming, because—like knowledge and understanding—ignorance and misinformation lead long lives.

A Princeton University study published in *Science Advances* in January 2019 concluded that while conservatives and Republicans disproportionately shared fake news online, the overwhelming predictor for careless media behavior was age. Authors Andrew Guess, Jonathan Nagler, and Joshua Tucker found that those aged sixty-five or above shared 7 times more fake news on Facebook than the youngest cohort, and 2.3 times more than those in the next oldest age group. This may point to the greater understanding by digital natives of the media ecosystem. It could point to GET OFF OF MY LAWN curmudgeonliness. But it certainly demonstrates that media illiteracy lasts a lifetime.

Once again, there are a lot of smart and well-meaning individuals and organizations on the case. You saw the impressive list. Just know that when you put a bunch of academics and civil-socialites on a committee and ask them to define the solution, as the Center for Media Literacy did, you get something like this:

> Media Literacy . . . provides a framework to access, analyze, evaluate, create and participate with messages in a variety of forms—from print to video to the Internet. Media literacy builds an understanding of the role of media in society as well as essential skills of inquiry and self-expression necessary for citizens of a democracy.

It's a perfectly good, suitably comprehensive definition, if you can reach the end still awake. It is surely a satisfactory starting point, but what it has yielded is a lot of negotiation, hemming and hawing, nitpicking, and general overcooking of curriculum that (a) doesn't necessarily penetrate the consciousness of the indifferent pupil, and (b) doesn't command much instructional time because it isn't math and the government doesn't mandate endless standardized testing on the subject.

I propose, therefore, a broader, complementary approach to media literacy education. I call it the Three Eights Plus One, and I envision it as sort of the Food Pyramid of media literacy. Or a do-it-yourself TrueCar that gives consumers the info they need to be empowered in the news showroom. It's three sets of fundamental questions that all citizens should be trained—and reminded of and reminded again—to apply to all ostensibly journalistic content, online and off.

The Three Eights Plus One can be distributed by the government, by news organizations, by libraries, by the PTA, by Facebook and Google, and by every other organization, institution, and private business with a stake in an informed public. Designed for approximately middle school to death, the checklists would look like this:

1. Where did this content come from?
2. Who is that person or organization?
3. Is it professional and credible?
4. Is it allied with a political or ideological viewpoint?
5. Have I ever heard of it? And, if not, have I Googled it? It's easy to make a website or a video look like a bona fide journalistic destination. Does this URL pass the smell test?
6. Is this news or content an outlier, or is it reported elsewhere by reputable sources?
7. Is this headline and content designed just to get my click, and the ad revenue that goes with it? Or does the information have intrinsic worth?
8. Does it seem designed to feed, pander to, exploit, or expand my worst suspicions about _____? Is it too good to be true, or too bad to be true?

OK. Like school and *Jeopardy!*, the questions get progressively harder. A related set of inquiries spins down from number 3 on the first list.

1. Do I know how credible information is produced and the process behind reputable reporting?
2. Are subjects dictated by fat-cat publishers? (Answer: no.)
3. Are they dictated by omnipotent editors flogging an agenda? (Answer: no.)
4. Do they follow marching orders of some outside third party, like advertisers, George Soros, the Trilateral Commission, the Bilderberg Group, the Freemasons, the United Nations, Big Pharma, the military-industrial complex, the Carlyle Group, or the Jews? (Answer: no.)
5. Are those anonymous sources invented by reporters to support a preferred narrative? (Answer: no.)
6. Is there a set of standard journalistic practices for confirming facts, qualifying sources, providing evidence, and immediately correcting errors? (Answer: yes.)
7. Do politically and ideologically funded and motivated players wrapping themselves in the audiovisual trappings of genuine news organization adhere to those standards? (Answer: often not.)
8. When politicians respond to criticism not by furnishing facts, evidence, or reasoned counterargument but by declaring "fake news," are they lying? (Answer: almost certainly.)

Those items cover the absolute basics. Toward a more intermediate-level ability to evaluate journalism, I'd add these:

1. Are assertions backed up—or challenged—by data, official records, history, or other documented evidence?

2. Is the audience given the sense of the sources' motives in saying what they say?

3. Is the reporter following the herd of other reporting, offering conventional wisdom provided with little scrutiny?

4. Are there signs that the elements of the story are the fruit of impartial inquiry, or do they seem cherry-picked to support a beginning hypothesis or narrative?

5. Is there evidence of bias toward controversy, versus less provocative but more substantial information?

6. Does the story fully contextualize statements and events to permit the audience to evaluate significance and meaning?

7. Is the reporting pointlessly speculative? Red flags are the words "may," "could," "should," "will."

8. Journalism can be slanted not just by what it includes, but by what it doesn't include. Are there holes in the reporting that suggest a conflicting narrative has been suppressed?

And, finally, the One: the overriding point that still eludes a good portion of the population, including the president of the United States: *Is the press permitted to criticize the government or its officials?*

Answer: Yes, for crying out loud, that is the entire point of a free press. It's in the First Amendment. To the Constitution. Ours.

Once again, these questions are not carved into stone tablets, and I am not Moses (for starters, I look like crap in sandals). So let educators quibble over the language. Let the experts design the presentation. But get it done, and let these checklists be spread far and wide. If they are in constant circulation at all information-consumer touchpoints, they will in time penetrate. They will become second nature. They will play havoc with the intentions of those who wish to play havoc with truth.

Maybe the Food Pyramid isn't a great analogy. (For one thing, it was shockingly unscientific and heavily influenced by the dairy lobby.) And maybe TrueCar is different, because those people ask all the skeptical questions for you. But however you think of it, the ingrained habit of media literacy is crucial to our democracy.

I should observe that Professor Greenwood of Montclair State makes a forceful argument that media literacy should not be stand-alone (and therefore marginalized) curriculum but rather an expression of general critical-thinking skills encouraged of students across the board. But why not both? The Three Eights Plus One are a template that applies equally to observation, problem solving, and intellectual rigor in any discipline and any context. If you export these basic tools of analysis to science, politics, even personal relationships you will be several steps closer to clarity of thought and, you know, enlightenment.

Hell, it can start with the movie ads. If you're shopping for entertainment, you don't want to plunk $12 down on a stinker. If you're shopping for governance or leadership or just plain reliable information, shouldn't you have the ability to detect a pack of fucking lies?

11

The Color Purple

This plank of the manifesto is about what we all should remember to remember, but I am obliged to begin with those things we must never forget.

Slavery, this nation's ur shame. The evil and its remnants are everlasting. It is an indelible stain on our history, but of course not the only one. The Trail of Tears. Vietnam. Tuskegee. Watergate. Internment of Japanese Americans during WWII. Overthrows in Chile, Iran, and the Dominican Republic. McCarthyism. Domestic spying. *Plessy v. Ferguson.* Nonexistent WMDs. The My Lai massacre. Abu Ghraib. Dresden. So many horrors perpetrated in the name of democracy, the worst moments in the application of power and the life of a nation. There are those in the world who believe these events define our nation. I believe they do not. What defines us is our acknowledgment of our sins, a determination to expiate them, a patriotic acceptance of the bedrock values and principles from which we have too often tragically strayed, and a desire to be, ultimately, a force of good. A shining example for the world.

Are we Jim Crow? Yes, but we are also the Civil Rights Act of 1964. Are we the nation of incarceration? Yes, and we are also the Miranda decision. Are we *Citizens United*? Yes, and we are also *Marbury v. Madison*—the foundational 1803 Supreme Court decision that vested the judiciary with authority to overturn laws and executive actions when they flout the Constitution.

We are distinguished by the Bill of Rights, civilian government, the rule of law, individual freedom, orderly transfer of executive authority, constant (albeit uneven) repair to the inequities and injustices flowing from entrenched power, and, historically at least, the beacon of hope, opportunity, and liberty we project to the tired, the poor, the huddled masses yearning to breathe free. In short: the American Way. Come on, you read all about this in history class, and also the comic books.

The American Way is what Superman fought for. It's what our troops have died for and what every elected official swears under oath to preserve. It is what our schoolchildren pledge allegiance to, however by rote they do so. These ideals are, in short, a nation's historical image of itself, the beating heart of our mythic American exceptionalism. We conduct ourselves without brutality in war. We open our arms to newcomers. We are a nation of laws, not men. And we are engineered by the founders to limit the power of the state—except (ironically enough) when it comes to upholding the *very Constitution that limits the power of the state*. They don't call it the Supreme Court for nothing.

You could argue that precisely that irony, or paradox, is at the center of our ongoing national identity crisis. Are we the heroic standard-bearers of the Four Freedoms, or are we the victims of a stolen way of life—pilfered by the very constitutional principles of liberty and justice for all? Remember when George H. W. Bush accused Michael Dukakis of being "a card-carrying member of the ACLU"? That's the American Civil Liberties Union, dedicated to advocating on behalf of the Bill of Rights. How did that ever become an insult? (For the depressing answer, go back to chapter 3.) Back in 2011, former House Speaker Newt Gingrich—supposedly the intellectual architect of the modern Republican Party but evidently unfamiliar with *Marbury*—said "activist" federal judges should be arrested by U.S. Marshals and jailed for decisions that eroded the power of the state. Jailed.

As for Make America Great Again—by undoing exactly what? If nearly half of the electorate is disgusted with how this whole democracy experiment has turned out, who are we? And how does this translate to the larger questions, for other individuals and American society as a whole? One must resist the temptation to be glib, but dare I suggest that the answer is hidden in plain sight? Never mind chapter 3. Have a look at our founding documents.

America was envisioned as a guarantor of respect for every individual's beliefs and desires and human rights within the context of the commonweal and our shared needs, as determined by the governments we elect and codified into law. Politics reflects the ebb and flow of those judgments, but must never be permitted to undo America's central promise: the sanctity of both the *pluribus* and the *unum*. To alter its exquisite balance is to deny the immutable essence of who we are. Which we used to know. With varying degrees of righteousness and mindless jingoism, it was drummed into our heads in history books, civics class, church, and almost everybody's political rhetoric. We believed we were exceptional. And My Lai didn't upend that belief; our national sense of horror at atrocities committed in our name cemented our core values. Because whether it was truly an anomaly or just a rare window into our worst reality, it *was not us.*

Our horror and disappointment were expressions of patriotism. How far we have sunk.

What passes for patriotism is now largely measured by the flag pins in our lapels and the mouthing of pride and faith in our soldiers, sailors, and aviators. Having long since lost track of the precepts of American democracy, we've devolved into a cult of military, with its own blind faith and liturgy, as mouthed by NFL announcers as the fighter planes fly overhead: "Quite a tribute to our men and women in uniform, who day in and day out sacrifice to defend our freedoms." In a time when objective facts and scientific consensus are politicized and debated as somehow controversial, it's odd that nobody ever asks, "Really? Which freedoms, exactly?" And why nobody ever approaches a federal judge in an airport to thank her for her service. Maybe that's because the federal judiciary, unlike the Pentagon, doesn't pay the NFL to promote its image.

So how ever to re-instill those timeless values, especially in a filter-bubble world? Tall order. One of the reasons we're in this fix, of course, is that the hyperfragmented media landscape offers no opportunity to reach everybody in one place. In that sense, one gets so nostalgic for 1964.

That's when a young woman was stabbed to death on the streets of Kew Gardens, Queens, New York. Her name was Kitty Genovese, and as the story was reported at the time, thirty-seven neighbors in surrounding apartments heard her screams and didn't so much as pick up the telephone to alert the police. The story turned out to be thin on corroboration, but nonetheless it captured the public's imagination and triggered a come-to-Jesus moment. Had we, as a society, become so isolated, so fearful, so selfish, so devoid of empathy that we would abdicate our most basic human responsibility to help a neighbor in peril? This became a national conversation. There was even a prime-time network special posing those very questions—because it was 1964, and that was possible. There were three networks. Three news magazines. *Life, Look*, and the *Saturday Evening Post*. A few thousand daily newspapers. In those days, when the situation demanded—whether a space shot, a Beatles tour, or a presidential assassination—you could coalesce a national conversation.

Not today. Not a war, not a mass shooting, not a Category 5 hurricane can command the public's attention for more than a news cycle or two. It's as if we are perpetually wading in the ocean surf. We're knocked down by a wave, and we right ourselves, only to be knocked over by the next. And the next. And the next, each tumble forgotten in the anxiety over what's coming. Because we are surely in 1964 no more. The handful of media institutions has been replaced with a nearly infinite number of channels, themselves channeled into our Facebook feeds and Google news platforms, where we are algorithmically served not a diversity of content and worldviews, but a constant stream of stuff we've demonstrated by our click behavior to enjoy. Estranged from non-affirming ideas, we have become a country of hostile tribes wedded to unquestioned tribal beliefs—all the while disconnected from the basic tenets (and triumphs) of democracy.

In the 1964 media-moderated encounter session, the nation asked if we'd become too isolated, and the answer was yes. So led by faith groups and civic institutions and political leaders and educators, we resolved to be, at least, better neighbors. But this is now.

How in this atomized world to discuss the threats to our democracy, and explain the function of our institutions, and tell stories about flesh-and-blood humans, and reignite America's fealty to the American Way? If you had a national two-hour prime-time show, it would reach maybe 2 percent of the population. But what if . . . what if we could amass a *virtual 1964*? What if someone could engineer a conspiracy of odd bedfellows, united by patriotism, casting party and ideology aside to excite Americans about America? Not to gloss over our many failings, but rather to highlight our triumphs.

Well, it's happening. It is called the Purple Project for Democracy, a vast, apolitical, nonpartisan campaign to reacquaint America with America-ness: hundreds of far-flung bastions of media, education, politics, and the arts representing the breadth of the nation, filling every screen, every publication, every classroom, every audio feed with stories of America by way of explaining—no matter what crap you find in your Facebook News Feed—how this government and the institutions of society work. Not how your subreddit tells you they work, but how they actually work and how they affect the lives of Americans every day. As this book is published, the first wave of Purple has just ended—a November 2019 campaign of content on television, radio, podcasts, newspapers, magazines, consumer advertising, libraries, town halls, social media, and, get this, Thanksgiving dinner tables throughout the land. (In the Great Thanksgivingtaking, the younger generation commandeered the program and replaced political squabbles with reflections on our freedoms.) All under the Purple banner. All of the above under the aegis of a broad coalition of major institutions representing the breadth of society, culture, business, education, and governance.

The theory: Every kernel of understanding dislodges one of misinformation, disinformation, or superstition. The hope: A blood transfusion for the body politic revives the moribund sense of national cohesion and purpose.

Now, it is abundantly clear that I myself have been radicalized by events of the past few years. When I discuss tribes, I am in one of them—the tribe that believes there is a horse loose in the hospital. So one might legitimately wonder how I can be an organizer of an apolitical initiative? Won't it be an explicit, or perhaps covert, campaign to brainwash the public with my disgust with the party in power? A Trojan horse for progressive doctrine and implicit repudiation of conservatism in all its forms?

Pleased to address that question: The answer is cross-my-fingers-and-hope-to-die no.

Why? Because though I have many failings, I'm not an idiot. I know the difference between a political crisis and a societal crisis, and I know the solution to the latter must not be infected by passions over the former. Not only have my fellow organizers and myself had *zero influence* on the content generated by the coalition of the willing, all participants have certified the content free of any partisan advocacy, policy advocacy, electoral ambition, or ideology whatsoever other than support for democratic institutions and values. Furthermore, the coalition behind Purple represents the entire population and political spectrum, tilting ever so slightly to the conservative side.

It is probably also fairly clear that such a ubiquitous campaign is impossible to organize and execute. The masterminds are a semi-retired business-school professor, a think tanker, a civic-engagement non-profiteer, and a talking head from public broadcasting. We among us have not the experience, the networks, or the resources to pull such a thing off. Alas, we are as a group too frightened to heed common sense. I think I speak for my colleagues when I say we feel as if we are witnessing a drowning twenty feet from shore, and we're stuck with a ten-foot rope. Which requires some swimming. Speaking for myself, I'll just say that I've been a journalist for forty years—which is to say, a battle-scarred veteran in the business of finding fault. But if at this stage of my career there is any chance to contribute something, anything, toward an actual solution, how can I not try?

How can any of us not try? How can we not pool our knowledge and our passion and our networks in the name of something so precious to our own nation and to the world?

There is, of course, an alternative, as exquisitely detailed by Edward J. Watts in his book *Mortal Republic*, about the gradual erosion of core values, democratic principles, and the welfare of the citizens when they are subordinated to political expediency, corruption, and the politics of fear. "When citizens take the health and durability of their republic for granted, that republic is at risk," Watts writes, adding, "a republic is a thing to be cherished, protected, and respected. If it falls, an uncertain, dangerous, and destructive future lies on the other side."

He wasn't guessing. The subtitle of Watts's book is *How Rome Fell into Tyranny*. It charts the Roman Republic from 323 B.C. to A.D. 14—from flourishing democracy constructed on division of power and rule of law to fourteen centuries of imperial tyranny, bloodshed, and decline. "Rome's republic died," he concludes, "because it was allowed to."

This manifesto, of course, is about intervention. And more on the means to follow, but first a few words about health insurance, drunken driving, individual philanthropy, and the internal politics of NPR. (Those things that are always, you know, totally bundled together.)

Let's start with insurance. If you are like most Americans, your health coverage is delivered through your employer and subject to varying degrees of choice, based on the composition of your family, level of coverage, changes in your life circumstances, and so on. Each year you or your heads of household have a forty-five-day period at the end of the year to make selections for the ensuing one. The same goes for Obamacare. The period is called "open enrollment." You go to a (secure) central platform, review your choices, update your dependents, and select your coverage accordingly. It's a bit of a chore, a bit of a contract, a bit of a ritual—for tens of millions of Americans every fall. File that idea away for a moment, please, and turn your attention to NPR.

It is a network, headquartered in Washington, D.C., where most of the programming—*Morning Edition, All Things Considered*—is produced and distributed. In addition to the in-house productions, it coproduces or distributes other favorites, such as *Fresh Air* (WHYY, Philadelphia), *Wait Wait Don't Tell Me!* (WBEZ, Chicago), *On Point* (WBUR, Boston), and others. *On the Media* for many years was one such program, but it is now self-distributed by our home station (WNYC, New York) as are *The Takeaway, The New Yorker Radio Hour,* and *Radiolab.*

A minority of the nine hundred stations in the public-radio ecosystem (which also includes American Public Media and Public Radio International) produces local content such as newscasts and talk shows. For the majority of markets, the news and information they hear on their local stations is entirely national programming. Thus, as a practical matter, in the digital age, for millions of listeners, at least as far as news and talk are concerned, the local broadcasters are functionally obsolete. Load an app on your phone and get all the national content in your earbuds on demand. Which is as impossible as it is logical, because (1) the local stations have coalesced a loyal audience for almost seventy years, (2) serving local—especially rural—audiences is a critical part of public broadcasting's mandate, (3) cutting them out of content distribution would quickly suffocate them, and (4) THAT'S WHERE ALL THE MONEY COMES FROM.

Contrary to the partisan mythology, government funding accounts for only 5.8 percent of public broadcasting's revenues, but at NPR, 37 percent of the budget comes directly from local stations. Technology or no technology, local broadcasters bring in the largest slice of the revenue pie and the lion's share of listeners through old-fashioned, terrestrial radio waves. The question of whether NPR headquarters or its component stations are more important, therefore, is a sort of chicken-and-egg scenario. Or goose-and-golden-egg scenario. Anyway, something with fowl and precious ova—bearing in mind that well-worn adage, in the search for truth, "follow the money." That approach tends to argue for the layers of the eggs.

But, once again, this is the digital age, governed increasingly not by radio tuners but by clicks and swipes. Obviously in this world, NPR must offer an app for one-stop shopping for its popular broadcasts and podcasts. But how to design such a thing when every click disintermediates nine hundred chickens? Aha! NPROne.

Have your phone handy? Go to the site one.npr.org. Now, where are you situated at the moment? If you are in Washington, D.C., like me, you are directed to WAMU-FM. If you are in Ames, Iowa, you're taken to WOI-FM. If you're in Mobile, Alabama, it's WHIL-FM. Magic! Based on your IP address, the app redirects you to your local station.

Got it? So now imagine an open-enrollment platform, as described above, with the geo-sensitivity to customize the page locally.

And now place that idea aside for a moment, too, as we consider philanthropy.

There was always philanthropy, which ebbed and flowed with the economy, the tax code, domestic and international episodes of calamity and hardship, the total pool of noblesse oblige, and levels of subtle and less-subtle social pressure—ranging from what your place of worship expected as a tithe, to what your fellow CEO shook you down for in $5,000-a-plate tickets to his favorite charity ball. Then, in 2012, Henry Timms, president and CEO of New York's 92nd Street Y, experimented with another force to bring to bear on the charity marketplace: the network effect. What if individual activity could be facilitated, and incentivized, online? Could generosity go viral?

Yep. Seven years later, Giving Tuesday generates hundreds of millions of dollars in forty-six countries of the world—$300 million (in 2017) in the United States alone. How? Because it combines a platform, a national event, and the expectation of participation that grows each year as the institution grows in awareness, collaboration, and sheer scale.

Now, finally, think about drunken driving.

In 2017, according to the Foundation for Advancing Alcohol Responsibility, the rate of DUI-related traffic deaths was 3.4 per 100,000 population. In 1981, it was 9.1 deaths per 100,000—an improvement of 63 percent. Why so steep a drop?

Part of the decline had to do with auto safety. Part flowed from wide awareness through the advocacy of Mothers Against Drunk Driving, which successfully lobbied for higher drinking ages and lower thresholds of blood-alcohol to trigger arrest. At the same time, the 1983 public-service-ad campaign "Friends Don't Let Friends Drive Drunk" implanted the notion of shared responsibility for reckless behavior, applying a social cost and just plain guilt feelings to the dynamic hitherto ruled by macho, misapplied "dignity," and reckless deference. The most precipitous drop in fatalities, however, correlates exactly with the introduction of the designated-driver concept. Following success in Scandinavia and Canada, the notion was exported to the United States in 1986 and quickly embraced by MADD, the Harvard School of Public Health, the beer and spirits industries, and the hospitality trade, not to mention Hollywood, which injected the notion of the designated driver in its TV plots and films. In a five-year span from 1988 (when the program went national) to 1993, the DUI fatality rate dropped by 20 percent. Because "designated driver" established a new societal norm and institutionalized the social penalty for defying it.

The difference in the fatality rate amounts to 18,240 Americans staying alive each year. That would be a sellout at the Las Vegas T-Mobile Arena.

Network effects. Societal norms. A national event. A geo-sensitive platform. Why shouldn't all these tried-and-true mechanisms be applied to instilling—or re-instilling—enthusiasm and commitment to our democratic institutions?

Rhetorical question. There is no reason why not. Because we know that, in theory, the desire is there. A spring 2018 survey by the Democracy Project—in association with Freedom House, the George W. Bush Institute, and the Penn Biden Center for Diplomacy and Global Engagement—asked Americans about their attitudes toward our democracy. Some of the most alarming findings were enumerated at the beginning of this book. But there was a significant silver lining. From the report:

> 81 percent endorse a proposal to provide "incentives for all young
> people to do public service, like military, teaching, or volunteer

work." The idea generated support from approximately 80 percent or more among most segments of the public, cutting across races, genders, age groups, political leanings, and education levels.

There is even stronger support for a proposal to "ensure that schools make civic education a bigger part of the curriculum." This is the single most popular initiative tested, with 89 percent favoring it as a way to bolster democracy.

And survey respondents were asked to evaluate this proposition: "Today, there is a great need for us all to act as responsible citizens—things like voting, volunteering, taking time to stay informed, and standing up for what's right—so that the freedoms and rights we cherish don't get whittled away."

With that notion before them, 86 percent expressed greater favorability with America's system of government. Unfortunately, that proposition is seldom, in any coordinated or systematic fashion, put before us. In other words, the heart is willing, but the infrastructure is weak.

So, in the wake of Purple, let's build the infrastructure. Let's construct a geo-sensitive platform that on, let's say, the first Wednesday after every first Tuesday in November, asks every citizen to log on and commit to some level of civic participation. It could be anything. Canvassing or otherwise helping a candidate in an election; volunteering at the library; testifying before an official board, council, or authority; running for office or seeking appointment to one of those official bodies; joining the PTA; lobbying elected officials or agencies on behalf of a policy; joining a neighborhood watch or roadway cleanup; making civic and media literacy part of church or Scout activities—whatever. It's open-enrollment day for democracy.

The same platform would, of course, stay in contact with you, encourage you, perhaps log your hours—à la Fitbit—and keep you informed of new opportunities. And naturally, when you enroll in your civic activity, it will notify your social graph on Facebook, Twitter, Instagram, and so on and award you a virtual purple flag sticker (or whatever), which would be emblazoned on your pages and your posts until you choose to turn it off. But why would you? Because you'd be proud. And if the purple flag weren't there? Well, maybe you'd be a little sheepish about that. Maybe just a little bit sheepish.

Because, as the man says, Americans don't let Americans opt out.

12

Coalition

"Kumbaya," the '60s expression of cheerful solidarity, has long since become a punch line for being trite and naïve. And sometimes it is both. But sometimes it is all-important.

Just look at how the impulse to factionalize has riven even the nominally single-minded women's movement. There was a time, for instance, when the word "feminism" gave you a pretty good head start as to the worldview of those who marched under its banner: equal rights, equal pay, escape from the yoke of male oppression at work and at home, and so on. Nowadays saying "feminism" is like saying "Iraq," nominally a country but in reality, just a set of political borders containing countless tribes, factions, sects, and subsects. A no doubt incomplete list, courtesy of St. Cloud State University's Cindy Moore: anarcho-feminism, cultural feminism, erotic feminism, eco-feminism, feminism and women of color, individualist or libertarian feminism, lesbianism, liberal feminism, Marxist and socialist feminism, material feminism, moderate feminism, pop-feminism, radical feminism, separatists.

The most recent fissure threatens the organization of the Women's March—the movement that grew out of the multi-city series of demonstrations in January 2017 in protest of Donald Trump's election. A 2019 march in Chicago never took place, ostensibly over cost concerns, but notably after national Women's March organizers were slow to condemn Chicago-based Nation of Islam leader Louis Farrakhan for anti-Semitic and homophobic rhetoric. "The powerful Jews are my enemy," he declared in February 2018, which elicited nary a peep from national Women's March leaders for a month—this even though national officer Tamika Mallory was in attendance when the slurs were unleashed. In time, the national organization disclaimed any tolerance for such bigotry.

"Minister Farrakhan's statements about Jewish, queer, and trans people are not aligned with the Women's March Unity Principles, which were created by women of color leaders and are grounded in Kingian Nonviolence," the organization posted on social media and its own website. "Women's March is holding conversations with queer, trans, Jewish, and Black members of both our team and larger movement to create space for understanding and healing.

"Our external silence has been because we are holding these conversations and are trying to intentionally break the cycles that pit our communities against each other. We have work to do, as individuals, as an organization, as a movement, and as a nation."

Laudable sentiments and a nice try to avoid the cycle of sectarian recrimination, but the damage was done. The California Women's March was canceled for fear that the crowds at the rally would be too white. Chapters in Rhode Island and Washington State announced plans to dissolve ties with the national organization.

"That sort of infighting within the movement is very painful," said Sara Kurensky, a board member for Women's March Chicago. "It's very painful to watch." Because, once again, there is danger in hyperfragmentation.

Now think about gender politics. You need a decoder ring. As our society becomes more awakened to gender fluidity, the alphabet designations begin to resemble the New York subway map. LGBT has given way to LGBTQ, QTPOC, QUILTBAG, and a whole glossary of permutations. It remains to be seen whether the alphabetization of self will ultimately be more enlightened, embracing, and liberating or anxiety creating, but mark me down for pessimistic. Assuming individual liberties are fully protected by law, you'd like to think it possible for the biologically binary and the sliding scale of gender identity to coexist without a constant argument. Alas, the signs are ominous. Consider the mind-bending conflicts that arise when feminist micro-identity butts heads with gender micro-identity, such as the nasty skirmishes between trans women and so-called trans-exclusionary radical feminists. Holy shit. *Don't you trespass on our feminist mommy blog, you uterus-less carpetbaggers! You are the advance army for "female erasure"!* One can only imagine where such disputes can lead, but I don't suppose a schism between vegetarian and vegan trans-exclusionary radical feminists can be too far away.

Maybe the most startling example came in March 2019, when actress and activist Alyssa Milano, in an expression of solidarity for the variously discriminated against, tweeted "I'm trans. I'm a person of color. I'm an immigrant. I'm a lesbian. I'm a gay man. I'm the disabled." How despicable, evidently. Instead of earning props for going all Spartacus on hostile tormentors, Milano was bombarded with criticism for so glibly, and without standing, expropriating the oppression of the genuinely oppressed. Here are some highly representative tweets of backlash:

> Had no idea you were a transgender. And you have the narcissism to think you can relate to everyone's life. No you're a white woman who feels that she needs to be ashamed so she takes on the role of hating herself to make sure no one hates her. Facts.

> No. No. This is not how any of this works. Oppression and intersectionality isn't an outfit that you decide to put on whenever you like.

> She's a rich elite who can't relate to the real world but gets high off of likes and retweets.

Hmm. Back in 2015, when a pair of Muslim radicals murdered twelve staff members of the French political satire magazine *Charlie Hebdo*, and millions around the world filled their social media feeds with the sympathetic slogan *Je suis Charlie Hebdo*, I don't recall any accusations of expropriating the tragedies of gunned-down satirists. But our grievances have become our possessions, our assets, so please keep your sticky, white, privileged, able-bodied, heterosexual fingers off our pain.

But put aside the particulars. The point here, in fact, *is* to sometimes put aside the particulars. Because while identity politics are useful for coalescing fellow travelers, addressing longstanding inequities, and crystallizing fundamental principles, they are also, by definition, extremely divisive. As the slicing of political and ethnic cohorts gets thinner and thinner, we edge closer and closer to the theoretical possibility that we will have eight billion people on earth in eight billion discrete groups of one. Which means very little consensus, *diminishing* tolerance, and an infinite opportunity for animosity. This phenomenon has been well documented by Todd Gitlin (1995), Michael Lind (1996), and notably Michael Tomasky in his 1996 broadside *Left for Dead*. Therein, he decried the shortsightedness and fundamental weakness of nanopolitics, writing that

> no member of any one of the left's defined groups has any obligation to those beyond the group: you needn't seek outsiders' cooperation or hear their opinions, because they're somehow inauthentic.... Not only are they inauthentic, but they're probably oppressors, particularly if they're white or male, intent on fooling you into further submission. What this means for the notion of a common culture, even a common working-class culture, is and has been disastrous.

The backlash to his dire conclusions pretty much made his point for him. "We have the white, male, heterosexual Tomaskys lecturing the rest of us about the relative unimportance of our issues ..." seethed historian and gay-rights activist Martin Duberman in 2002. Nobody, of course, wants to be slighted or condescendingly dismissed, but Duberman's impulse to defend the political wisdom of infinite splintering by dismissing his critics as just too hegemonic to possibly understand ... well, QED.

Among those who have observed this phenomenon with horror is the conservative pundit Andrew Sullivan:

> When elite universities shift their entire worldview away from liberal education as we have long known it toward the imperatives of an identity-based "social justice" movement, the broader culture is

in danger of drifting away from liberal democracy as well. If elites believe that the core truth of our society is a system of interlocking and oppressive power structures based around immutable characteristics like race or sex or sexual orientation, then sooner rather than later, this will be reflected in our culture at large.

Obviously, societal progress and justice demand that some architecture of entrenched power be torn down, Berlin Wall–like. The civil rights movement has righteously dismantled much of the superstructure of racial discrimination. The #MeToo movement is gradually undermining male impunity over sexual harassment and worse. But not all identity subtleties are the stuff of oppression, and not all structures need to be leveled. We are so awash in trigger warnings, safe spaces, and microaggressions—an ever-growing code of conduct applying to an ever-growing catalogue of human interactions—I can't help but think of the U.S. Postal Service.

On August 20, 1986, an Edmond, Oklahoma, postal employee named Patrick Sherrill went on a shooting rampage that killed fourteen coworkers and injured six others. Over the next decade, in nine other incidents, similar horrors struck the nation's post offices, claiming twenty-four lives. Apart from the obvious derangement of the individual killers, the act of "going postal" was attributed to the vast, inflexible body of government work rules that deprived individuals of agency, discretion, and their very identities. They felt, in short, not only emasculated but dehumanized. Too many rules. Too little agency. Of such rage little good can come.

I was recently given a heads-up by a theater colleague whom I very much like and respect that possibly my use of the salutation "ladies and gentlemen" may be too freighted with presumption and therefore subtly or not so subtly oppressive. "Let me give that some thought," I said. I don't claim that there aren't those situated in various places across the gender spectrum for whom the convention doesn't strictly apply. But if I may be blunt: Women are being raped by their dates and bosses. Black men and boys are being harassed and gunned down by police. We have to, at this point in time, choose our battles. There are bigger fish to fry.

One argument, of course, states that there is no level of inequity too small to be addressed, and redressed. Another argument says that countless micro-grievances yield little sympathy, but instead a visceral rejection of and backlash against "political correctness," which affects not only the "stamp out ladies-and-gentlemen" movement, but also urgent, crucial, life-and-death issues such as #MeToo and Black Lives Matter. In other words, beware the blowback of the Child-Who-Identifies-As-Male Crying Wolf.

And, once again, micro-identity leads to the creation of a highly visible Other. Think of the peacock. Do the benefits of finding and flaunting yourself always justify the risk of attracting predators?

There is more at stake here than Procter & Gamble figuring out you have eczema and a Vietnamese novelist elbowing Jane Austen out of the canon. Because long before political, gender, and ethnic identity got fragmented into micro-cohorts, political parties, nationalist movements, and revolutionary insurgencies battled for power based on broad but nonetheless inflexible doctrine—doctrine that surely bound individuals together in common cause but reciprocally identified and targeted enemies. And the history of such identity conflict is the history of war, pogroms, genocide, and every conceivable violent expression of man's inhumanity to man. Of particular (and tragically recurring) danger is ethno-nationalism, which has the fearsome quality of pitting a majority population against literally everyone else perceived to threaten power or racial/religious/

linguistic homogeneity, traditions, and values. History offers numerous ghastly examples, dating to the earliest civilizations, among them the destruction of Carthage by the Romans in 149 B.C., the extermination of the Chinese minority Wu Hu in the fourth century A.D., the Spanish Inquisition, and our very own 100 percent American Trail of Tears. But nationalism is the gift that keeps on giving. Nazism, the Armenian genocide, the Mideast conflict between an increasingly apartheid Israeli state and a surrounding majority widely wishing for its eradication, Rwanda, Greater Serbia, and the Balkan Wars—all horrors of the past century. In Myanmar right now, after decades of convulsive politics, the Rohingya Muslims are being wiped out in full view of the world.

Conversely, when minority Others mobilize, they identify an Other, too, in the body of the ruling majority, and of such asymmetry comes separatist movements that—when political means fail—have often resorted to violence, including terrorism. The Irish Republican Army. The Tamil Tigers. The Basque ETA. The Chechen resistance movement. The PLO. The Kurdish PKK. It's a long list. Mind you, I'm not suggesting any individual or group should tolerate oppression. The American Revolution, after all, was pretty righteous (not to mention anticolonial movements in Asia, Africa, and South America that turned the nineteenth-century status quo upside down). What I am saying is that we cannot discuss identity without discussing life-and-death conflict of sometimes staggering proportions and which can set entire societies ablaze. Beginning, even, with tiki torches. The Pittsburgh synagogue massacre followed by only a year.

I spoke of fragments—identity groups organized largely by grievance—and how the society has been torn asunder, each constituency militantly protecting parochial interest at the expense of the commonwealth. But I also invoked Abraham Lincoln and his bundle of sticks. Individually they are easily snapped in two. As a bundle, they are unbreakable. The future of American democracy is to bundle, to coalesce, to march arm in arm in defense of shared interest and shared values and shared resolve. In fact, on the subject of Lincoln, it's useful to remember the words of one of his Civil War officers, Major General Nathaniel P. Banks. He was the military viceroy in charge of the occupied state of Louisiana, charged with enforcing an unpopular presidential decree for establishing a restoration government. For reasons of timing and political expediency, Lincoln had decided—against all apparent logic and justice—to deny blacks a vote in the election of the new governor. The black suffrage was to be granted after the new government was formed, but needless to say, both free blacks and white Unionists in the vanquished confederate state wigged out. Banks, as author Steve Luxenberg documents in his book *Separate*, dismissed the criticism as immorally unpragmatic. "When the national existence is at stake," he said, "and the liberties of the people are in peril, faction is treason."

While "treason" might be a tad hyperbolic, factionalism certainly weakens structures. Yes, the society has atomized, but atoms are by definition constituent parts of much bigger things. Worlds. Ballot boxes. The beating hearts of future generations.

We must act, and comrades, so we shall. Not to be revolutionaries imposing some other utopian political system on our nation, but to rediscover and embrace what we have. To take to the streets, marching not under the Purple banner, but the American flag. To be born again in democracy. To dance with who brung us. To not throw the baby out with the bathwater. To reassemble the intricate puzzle of our *pluribus*es—into our exquisitely fragile *unum*.

Let me offer an optimistic coda from the earlier-discussed Robbers Cave Experiment.

You'll recall that placing a population of young boys in a state park and arbitrarily dividing them into two groups—the Eagles and the Rattlers—led to a *Lord of the Flies*–like regression into tribal enmity and violence. Having observed the effects of schism, the researchers then contrived to break down the barriers of resentment and distrust by engineering joint activities, such as a movie night, bean-collecting contest, and fireworks shooting. This did not lead to any appreciable reconciliation. It did lead to several food fights.

(Do keep that in mind when people say the way to reunite Red and Blue America, by gosh, is just to get everybody talking to one another. We're not so different! Alas, as we have seen, it doesn't require a very big difference to foment an argument. Or a genocide.)

But then the researchers wondered, what if they could get the kids not just to co-participate, but to actually cooperate? To bring them together not to set off skyrockets, but to deal with several issues that neither group could address alone. "Superordinate goals," sociologists call them. One was to free a food-delivery truck—that is, delivering food for the whole camp—from a deep rut in the dirt road. Another was to choose a movie, which the kids would have to help pay for, even though one team would have to pay slightly more per person than the larger rival. A third was to find the source of a cut-off water supply and repair it. When the flow resumed, the group outfitted with canteens gave way to the thirstier group without them. When the camp ended, by their own vote, the Rattlers and the Eagles chose to return home in the same bus. And along the way, the team that had won $5 in the bean-collecting contest used the money to buy malted milks for everyone. Project Purple is the ultimate superordinate goal, casting aside parochial interests and grievances toward a common imperative.

Like the alt-right, minus the evil.

We can hold our heads in despair, or we can repair what has been put asunder. Wishful thinking, you say? Pollyanna, you say? Totally fucking delusional, you say? No. It can be done. In any event, when there is a life at stake, smug dismissiveness is not an option. Only resuscitation. Long live democracy. Long live this traumatized but noble Dumpty.

Conclusion

I t's a bracing winter's day, early in 2019, at the Arlington National Cemetery.

The chill in the air and windy gusts are softened by the sun, which is untroubled by the wisps of cirrus clouds streaking the sky. At the eternal flame for John F. Kennedy, the American flag snaps against the breeze on the hill just below the Custis-Lee Mansion. Below, the gravesite's dramatic northern vista is a postcard tableau of the nation's capital. The Washington Monument. The U.S. Capitol. The Lincoln Memorial. But of course nearer to this vantage—in fact, enveloping it—is a more sacred monument to our democracy: the 624 acres of headstones, row on row, that mark the memories, the sacrifices, and the final resting places of so many. James Tanner. Scip Tate. Billy Bob Walkabout, Felix Z. Longoria Jr., Kareem Rashad Sultan Khan, Winifred Collins, Saburo Tanamachi, Alejandro L. Manriquelozano, Uday Singh, Rene Gagnon, Olavi Alakulppi,

Luther Skaggs Jr., Nino Dugue Livaudais, Zdzislaw Bruno Kadle-wicz, Ivica Jerak, Benni Goldblatt. They all did their duty. Some served with devotion. Some with distinction. Some with valor. None of them was on the *Mayflower*.

A plain, white marker for all of them, irrespective of rank or station. It is a grim, proud orchard of Georgia marble. And all I can think of, as I guide a young Japanese visitor around the cemetery, is that in 2019, American ideals are better represented by the dead than by the living.

Before we finish our tour, we linger a bit in the visitor center, a small-scale museum documenting the history of the place. One of the exhibits is a photograph from Armistice Day, November 11, 1918, documenting a vast celebration in downtown Philadelphia to commemorate the end of World War I. Nearly five million Americans served in Europe. More than 116,000 never returned—a horrific death toll in itself, but almost a rounding error in a war that claimed thirty-seven million human souls, 2 percent of the population of the entire world.

For two years, in the face of such unimaginable butchery, a largely isolationist United States delayed its entry. In time, economic interests, German attacks on our shipping, sympathy for our British cousins, and just plain moral imperative converged to change the calculus. But I've often wondered how the public came to accept and even embrace the mission, and the sacrifice it entailed. We were, after all, sending our boys into a bloodbath, and the Hun wasn't headed here. It was a gut check to end all gut checks in the "war to end all wars." If ever our values as a nation were put on the line, it was there, but what values were they, exactly; what did we finally agree was at stake?

I stared at the photo of the teeming streets of Philadelphia. The city fathers had erected a monument there, a temporary one, to preside over the celebration. It was scaled down but nonetheless soaring, the Statue of Liberty in replica. She who stands in New York Harbor, as a guardian of our own way of life and a beacon for the world. She is why our boys went. She is who they fought for. She is for whom they died. She is the great symbol not of their sacrifice, but of their shared ethos. She is the idea buried beneath the white slabs of marble.

And here we are again, struggling not with foreign enemies but with domestic rot. What about now? Shall we rally around Lady Liberty? Shall we? What if we do not?

ACKNOWLEDGMENTS

I t takes a village—a village of generous suckers willing to provide support and actual labor, usually without compensation,
in support of someone else's self-indulgence. I'm grateful, therefore, for the expert review of early-draft pages by Allesandro Acquisti, Jim Anderson, Jason Kint, Joe Mandese, Vanessa Greenwood,
Charlie Penner, Randall Rothenberg, and Steve Smith, whose cu-
mulative grasp of certain technical subjects exceeds mine by several
orders of magnitude. Roger McNamee's Silicon Valley–eye–view
was invaluable. And his book *Zucked: Waking Up to the Facebook
Catastrophe*—one of dozens of published sources I've drawn from
to support my arguments—nonetheless stood out for its insight and
detail. A special shout-out to Doug Stauffer of *Media Matters*, whose
vast archive of documented Fox News Channel outrages was infu-
riatingly useful.

I've benefited almost obscenely from the unflagging moral

support of Misha Collins, Milena Garfield, Chris George, Tyler Parkinson, and Steve Rosenbaum, who have been with me on this every step of the way.

Endless thanks to the current production team at *On the Media*: Alana Casanova-Burgess, Asthaa Chaturvedi, Leah Feder, Jon Hanrahan, and Micah Loewinger, who every week generously share their extraordinary scope and boundless curiosity on the very matters considered herein, and also to former *OTM* producer Sara Qari, who produced a piece that significantly informed chapter 4. My cohost and editorial lodestar, Brooke Gladstone, is my daily inspiration for inquiry, clarity, rigor, and cutting ~~superfluous~~ adjectives. *OTM* executive producer Katya Rogers is the visionary/air traffic controller/ therapist who not only miraculously manages the five-alarm neediness of her hosts, but harnesses the energy week after week to power our show. Ever skeptical, she is also ever understanding, and has consistently given me wide berth to advance my extracurricular adventures. The same goes for Andrew Gollis and Jim Schachter, current and previous WNYC bosses of my boss, who have lent me their support while heroically not firing me.

My agent, Jane von Mehren of Aevitas, is an unsurpassed focuser of mushy authorial thinking and expert maker of publishing matches. It was she who brought me together with Counterpoint Press, and I'm so glad she was there to preside over the marriage. At Counterpoint, production editor Jordan Koluch created a marvelously retro look to lend the texture of gravitas to my ravings. She also guided an astonishingly buttoned-up copyediting and proofreading process. I cannot overestimate the importance of that undertaking, as I have some glaring weaknesses in matters of typing and, you know, thinking.

As such, I owe a particular debt to Dan Smetanka, Counterpoint editor in chief, who, in varying degrees of gentleness, challenged me to apply discipline to a form—polemic—not especially noted for its restraint or its rigor. He generously embraced my premise from the outset, but also demanded consistency of argument, and prevented me from straying from the topic at hand. A manifesto ultimately is a document of desperation. Dan never let my desperation veer out of its lane.

© Andrew French

BOB GARFIELD is the cohost of WNYC's weekly Peabody Award–winning *On the Media*. Garfield has been a columnist and contributing editor for *The Washington Post Magazine*, *The Guardian*, and *USA Today*, as well as an author, lecturer, podcaster, and broadcast personality on ABC, CBS, CNBC, PBS, and NPR. He lives in suburban Washington, D.C. Learn more at www.bobgarfield.net.

Printed in the United States
by Baker & Taylor Publisher Services